Who We Met on the Way to Stanford

A Father's Memoir

Richard P. Sinay

ISBN (hardcover): 978-1-959555-12-4
ISBN (paperback): 978-1-959555-07-0

PLATYPUS
PUBLISHING

To Tina, for her love and support throughout the writing.

To Heidi and Jennie, who sacrificed as well.

To Lin-Manuel Miranda, for the inspiration.

To All Parents dedicated to their aspiring athlete.

Contents

Preface

I was rummaging through my writings on my computer and came across a folder from my son, Brian. When I took a look inside, I found a set of notes he had sent me in his junior year of college, asking me to help him draft a letter to a scholarship committee. When I rediscovered the notes, I felt like the narrator in "The Custom House," the introductory short story to the novel *The Scarlet Letter* by Nathaniel Hawthorne, who had discovered an embroidery of the scarlet letter "S." I thought how ironic it would be for me to use this moment as the foundation for writing. As it turned out, it was. I delved deeply into the history of the notes he had sent me and spent countless hours researching the data. This is how my book came about.

The book came into being to fully understand this episode in the life of my son, myself, and my family. All of us were affected by it, and all of us sacrificed for the achievement. In a way, for me, it was part therapy and part discovery of what I feel to be the closest to the truth of the matter that I could get. It is my memoir, and it is my point of view, yet I understand others involved may have differing points of view. It does not matter what others may think. This is how I understood things as a father who knew his son better than anyone.

At one point in my golf career, I arrived at almost a zero handicap, and so the learning I did during the growth of my son's golf skill gave me a game I still love to play. Teaching my son also allowed me to know a lot about golf while meeting some of the greatest golfers of all time. This is how the book came to exist.

Introduction

"Then the carousel started, and I watched her go round and round...All the kids tried to grab for the gold ring, and so was old Phoebe, and I was sort of afraid she'd fall off the goddam horse, but I didn't say or do anything. The thing with kids is, if they want to grab the gold ring, you have to let them do it and not say anything. If they fall off, they fall off, but it is bad to say anything to them."

Holden Caulfield, *The Catcher in the Rye*

There is irony in life. I know. I've been there. Ironic things happen when a person works so hard for something and then doesn't get it; it is the ultimate cruelty of life. I suppose the worst recent example is that of Hillary Clinton, who had her hands on the Golden Ring, and then she fell and couldn't hold onto it. I know it in my own life when not chosen for college jobs I was far more qualified for than the person who got it. Sometimes important things turn out a lot differently than I expected, and the resultant irony of life comes to pass.

This memoir is about how my son got to Stanford on a golf scholarship and what happened when he got there. This memoir teaches us that setting goals and reaching them are two different things. While I did my best as a father to help my son achieve a goal, he had set for himself in the sixth grade, I could not do anything but watch the dynamics of what went on when he got to Stanford to play golf for the scholarship he received. This story is for all those parents who put their heart and soul into making their young golfer good enough to play on professional tours. It is a universal story of trial and tribulation and all that goes into making a young player of any sport achieve ultimate success. This story is about one of those players who had extraordinary talent and achieved great success as a junior golfer.

I will tell the story of who my son and I met along the way to achieving my son's goal. Golf is an excellent community because having success in it brings significant people into one's life. Along the way, golf would include the likes of Jack Nicklaus, Gary Player, Tiger Woods, Hunter Mahan, Aaron Baddeley, Kevin Na, Lorena Ochoa, James Oh, Sean O'Hair, John Merrick, Sergio Garcia, Ty Tryon, J.J. Killeen, Chris Tidland, Steve Conway, Ron Won, and Jim Seki. The reader may not know all these names, but once finished with the book, they will learn more about who they are. During our travels around the country and three trips to Japan to play in The Japan Cup, we encountered all of these players in one capacity or another. I will weave the stories into my reflection on my time raising a gifted young golfer.

Throughout this memoir, there will be many times when amazing things happen, including breaking Tiger Woods' high school record; Jack Nicklaus' incredible shot at Dove Canyon Country Club; Sergio Garcia playing two rounds of golf with my son; the astonishing story of a little lady from Guadalajara, Mexico; the rugged beginnings of a young golfer named

Hunter Mahan, and a round of golf with famed Yankee baseball player Reggie Jackson.

When Tiger Woods competed in high school, he won three high school championships in Southern California, a feat as extraordinary as his three US Junior Amateur wins. My son, Brian Sinay, had a couple of chances to tie that remarkable record. Although he came close, newspaper articles were comparing the two accomplishments. Because Brian had the singular focus of wanting to play golf at Stanford, it was assumed he wanted to follow in the footsteps of Tiger Woods. Although partly true, Brian's drive and determination to get a scholarship to Stanford is only part of the story. These and other stories are my memories of teaching and playing golf with my son, Brian.

This book is also about what happened when Brian arrived at Stanford and the story behind achieving his goal; expectation and loss; achieving goals; life; and the ironies it sometimes brings. All of these players in this story except one had the dream of playing on the PGA Tour, but for some, it was more the father's dream that this would happen for their sons. Every player discussed in this memoir was chasing the "Golden Ring." Arriving on the PGA Tour is grabbing the "Golden Ring." For Brian Sinay, that was never the intent of his passionate pursuit of golf. He had one goal: to get a scholarship to Stanford and play where Tiger Woods and Tom Watson played golf in college. And, at the same time, get a good college education.

Throughout the time we played golf, there was no discussion about what Brian would do to get to the PGA Tour. The first several years of golf were all about getting better, playing in local competitions, and seeing how he would measure up to other players. The first goal was to get better until one day, he had a conversation with a fellow golfer when they were in the sixth grade. His name was Steve Conway, and he and Brian both grew up in Irvine, CA, where privileged kids came from. The conversation would establish a new goal for Brian as a golfer, and it was a pivotal point in Brian's life with golf.

It established a challenge for him, and Brian was always up for it. When Brian was in second grade, his teacher started a reading contest called "The Snowball Blitz" to see who could read the most books in a given amount of time. We, as parents, were amazed to see Brian walking around the house with a book in his hands, reading. And he read and read and read, and eventually, he won the contest by a long shot. While I cannot recall the number of pages, it was pretty substantial. It established several things for him: he was an obsessive-compulsive kid and always up for a challenge. He loved to compete. He loved to win. He loved the rewards of winning.

This memoir will take us from year to year in Brian's life as he grew up and learned golf. It will also include what I learned. The purpose is to show how much dedication it takes to be good enough to earn a scholarship to a major university like Stanford. This game of golf is just as it is with any sport: it takes profound dedication to achieve that goal. Most people who have dedicated themselves to pursuing any sport will not know what it takes to get to the major leagues, play in the NBA, or arrive on the golf course as a player for the PGA. People may think that these are just gifted athletes, and they were born that way. In some respects, that is true, but for the most part, even a "gifted" athlete must work hard at the game to be the best he can be. Most of us know the dedication of Kobe Bryant, who pushed others to work hard despite already being an NBA superstar. Most of us know the extraordinary efforts of Tiger Woods. It is beyond what most people can imagine.

This memoir's second part will take us through what happened at Stanford when Brian arrived in the fall of 2000. I will narrate the incidents based on feedback from Brian and some of my conversations with the other players. I also received a set of notes that Brian made to capture his experience playing for Coach Jeff Mitchell at Stanford. Writing this is challenging because it brings back memories of what happened. Golf is replete with the stories of "flameouts," players who had great promise yet never delivered on that promise. This book is also a memoir of those who "flamed out" as they reached for the "Golden Ring" of being a consistent player on the PGA Tour. It is the story of one young man who, like many of the others we will encounter in the memoir, managed to "flame out" before the others. It is written in retrospect many years after the actual incident, but sometimes years of distance make for a better understanding of what happened. In it, we will find when players who went for the PGA found themselves unable to compete for reasons we may never know, and we just know that they didn't make it. We will learn about how many players look to become PGA Tour players and how many of them fall short of the goal of grabbing and holding onto the "Golden Ring."

Chapter 1: 1985-1988

Tiger Woods and Hitting Golf Balls in Diapers

"When Tiger was six months old, he would sit in the garage, watching me hit balls into the net. He had been assimilating his golf swing and had a golf swing when he got out of the highchair."

Earl Woods

We golfers all know the story of Tiger Woods appearing on the Mike Douglas show at the age of three. His dad wanted to show everyone how "great" he was as a three-year-old. We all know that parents see their kids differently than others do, but apparently, Earl Woods saw more in that kid than we did at such a young age. Tiger's first swing lesson was watching Dad swing a golf club in the garage as he sat in his highchair. In a sense, Tiger Woods was swinging a golf club when he was in diapers. We know that time spent manipulating that club has much to do with learning to control that ball. By the time he was three years old, he had a swing that looked pretty good, which he demonstrated on the Mike Douglas Show.

Tiger's story is well known to golfers: he won tournaments at a very young age against more senior players, winning the Junior World Golf Championship in San Diego when he was eight years old against nine- and ten-year-olds. As an eight-year-old child, he said he did not use more than a pitching wedge on most of the holes at the Presidio Golf Course in Old Town San Diego. He won many tournaments in the Southern California Junior Golf Association all over the Southern California region. Before long, he won his first U.S. Junior Amateur, and then another, and another. No one had done that before.

He followed those victories with three U.S. Amateur wins, and nobody had done that either. He added an NCAA Individual Championship to his ever-growing list of wins. Tiger went out on tour and won right away, and without repeating the details of all fifteen of his majors, he has also won eighty-three PGA Tour events. And he started hitting when he was in diapers.

I only tell the story of Tiger because he is linked to my son Brian. When he was twelve, Brian met Tiger and received the Player of the Year award from the Southern California Junior Golf Association for winning several tournaments. In the fall of that year, Tiger went to Stanford. When Brian won the high school championship in his first year in high school and then repeated as champion again when he is a junior in high school, he was linked to Tiger. He had a chance to equal a record that Tiger had set by winning the Southern California High School Championships three times. Brian's interest in attending Stanford to play golf for them was also a connection to Tiger, who had gone there. Brian was never described as the next Tiger Woods because Tiger had not yet proven himself at the highest levels of golf.

When I started teaching my son to play the game, it was not because I wanted him to grow up and be a PGA Tour player, even though that is the dream of most fathers. It was not mine, never was, and it was not the intent from the beginning to make him one. I wasn't even a good player at golf, practically knowing nothing about the proper techniques for the different aspects of golf: chipping, pitching, sand play, and putting. It was all about just having fun playing together and bonding. I did not know that my kid would take to it so well that he quickly became much better than anyone might expect. For that to happen was both fun and gratifying, but there was still no intent on him grinding away to play on the PGA Tour eventually. There was no goal for his efforts, or mine, for a while. Becoming a better player at golf became more of a priority than looking into the future of his golf goals.

By the time Brian was in kindergarten, he was a "veteran" of swinging the plastic golf club and bashing the Wiffle ball around the house. It comes with the territory that anyone who became a great player started at an early age. In those early years, Brian spent a good deal of time on putting greens at Rancho San Joaquin Golf Course in Irvine.

He was just three years old when we moved to Irvine. We had rented a house for about a year, waiting for a new home to be built. We bought the house in September 1984 and moved in April 1985. Here, Brian would learn the game of golf with practice sessions at the local public golf courses: Rancho San Joaquin and Newport Beach Golf Course, an eighteen-hole executive golf course.

Aside from the occasional golf practice and playing, soccer and baseball were the two other sports that he enjoyed playing.

Each fall season would mean playing on another soccer team. Each spring season would suggest playing on another baseball team, and playing other sports was important because I never had the mindset, like other dads, just to make the kid focus on one sport. Even Jack Nicklaus played other sports when he was growing up, and it didn't stop him from achieving greatness in golf. Not allowing a kid to play other sports is "stealing" a bit of childhood away from them. That goes with the singularity of playing one sport perpetually and perhaps even giving up playing with other kids in the neighborhood. What kind of childhood is that?

I played golf from time to time during these years, but I could have been better. I did not know a great deal about golf in those days. Five years later, in the spring of 1990, we decided to join a country club to play more golf. I had already started to read books about playing the game of golf but never realized that it was as complicated as it was. There are many subtleties to the game, and it would be long before I learned what they were. As I read things, I taught Brian and myself. I stood in the foyer of the house and taught myself the swing by repeating a pattern taught to me by David Leadbetter in his book *The Golf Swing*. From his book, I was able to teach Brian the fundamentals of the game, and he took to it quite naturally.

He was able to hit balls when he was in kindergarten because he had already repeated the motion many times with his plastic golf club swing. He hit balls well right away. When we turned to the short game, especially putting, it also came naturally as he had had several hours on the putting green from when he was five years old. This early training and experience helped him develop a great touch around the greens. Allowing a kid to learn the feel of the game at a very young age has benefited a lot of players. It enables the kid to be successful early in their play, making the game a gratifying experience.

Parents bring their unprepared kids to Tee-Ball (I coached for several years). Sometimes the kid does not even know how to put on a baseball glove! I suppose the assumption on the part of the parent is that they are there to learn how to put on a glove, how to hold a bat, and how to swing. It never dawned on them that perhaps some of that training could take place at home before sending the kid to Tee-Ball. For some strange reason, parents think the child is too young to swing a bat, swing a plastic golf club, throw a ball, or catch a ball. When Brian and his sister Jennie were two, I threw a ball at them, and they developed their catching skills. It isn't rocket science, but some parents don't know how to teach their kids.

Getting serious about golf was still far away, but there was always time for it. It was our summer sport and the activity that took place whenever we had time between baseball games. Baseball would run from the spring into the summer, and eventually, the two sports would collide. It would be a while before that happened. So those early years were more about playing team sports with the kids in neighborhood leagues, having fun developing the skills to play soccer and baseball, and then turning to golf when the occasion arrived. Brian and his sister Jennie did a lot of team sports in the early days. It was fun and hilarious at the same time watching all the kids on the soccer field bunched around the ball and each of them trying to get a kick at it. For Brian, golf was not a big deal; it would be a while before it was.

Chapter 2: 1989

Kevin Na and Learning the Golf Swing

"Courage is the resistance to fear, mastery
of fear-not the absence of fear."

Mark Twain

Brian devoted the time in the summer when he wasn't playing another sport to getting better at golf. I did not have anyone work with Brian at this age (eight years old) because I did not think it was a big deal. I did not make a big deal about golf because I was ignorant of what the early preparation to play golf was like for some of the best players. The neglect in teaching him how to play golf was more because I did not know his talent then, and I never had the intent that he would become a professional golfer. The purpose of playing golf was to have fun together and enjoy playing the game, and I had no expectations and no idea that he would be a good player.

The question of whether a good golfer is born or made is

not that unsettled. Players are gifted with athletic abilities that come from the genetics they are born with, but they allow their athletic ability to improve with practice like any other skill. However, even with these physical talents and practice, the player still has to work hard to learn the game's nuances.

Malcolm Gladwell popularized the 10,000-hour rule in his best-seller *Outliers*. In the book, Malcolm argues that "it takes about 10,000 hours of intensive practice to achieve mastery of complex skills and materials." Whether playing the piano or a violin or mastering the complexities of hitting, chipping, pitching, or putting a golf ball, a great deal of time needs to be put in for mastery. It has been argued that Tiger Woods had done so by age twelve. It may have been why he would win three US Junior Amateur Championships, three US Amateur Tournaments, and an NCAA Individual Championship. I did not know about the 10,000-hour rule early in the golf development of Brian Sinay. I also did not realize that good instruction was integral to better growth by the player as well. But as I saw his talent emerging with his putting and striking the golf ball, I felt it was necessary to start reading seriously about what one had to do well in this game. Little did I know that it can take thousands of hours of study to know the golf swing and to understand the subtle techniques of each part of the game.

This 10,000-hour rule has since been overshadowed by studies that indicate that both practice and good instruction are needed to improve. I can attest to this with my son, Brian, who did a tremendous amount of practicing without the desired results. It was when I turned to the books on golf instruction that allowed me to teach him the skills through the education I received from the likes of Butch Harmon, David Ledbetter, and Hank Haney. While I was not a very good golfer when instructing my son, I could have been more informed than I was from my reading. Because his golf instruction was exclusively on the golf swing, I needed to learn as much as I could from the books on the short game. I had to learn about pitching, putting, sand play, and chipping to help him improve to a higher level of player. I read as many books as possible on the short game but reading a book was different from putting in the time as a player and discovering the subtleties of each of those skills.

A lot of time was spent at the driving range hitting golf balls. Hitting at the range went on for two or three years, and time improved the ball striking. Brian began to figure out ball striking himself by "digging it out of the dirt," as Hogan referred to it. It would not be until the following year when David Leadbetter's book *The Golf Swing* was published that I was able to give more proper instructions to Brian about how to strike the golf ball. Despite reading the book, I was still not the expert that someone like Tiger would be teaching his own kid to play.

Getting better instruction was going on all over the country with players whose parents were PGA Tour players or PGA Teaching professionals. I was the other way around as a Dad who attempted to teach his son when I really didn't know squat about it. I was one of those Dads who thought it was some-thing I could teach. But it made it hard to have credibility with the kid when Dad doesn't know what he's talking about.

Perhaps this is a fair warning to Dads who might read this narrative: teaching the kid the fundamentals of golf should be left to the experienced professional. I also have to say that not all PGA professionals are automatically good teachers or have a great understanding of the golf swing. A Dad must know whether the PGA instructor has successfully taught players before turning his kid over to them for instruction. I learned this long after my son was involved with golf when it was too late.

The cruel irony of golf is that one can put in a lot of hours doing the wrong thing. I was determined to at least know the game's sound fundamentals, even if I didn't know the complexities of the golf swing. But making it fun was what we did in those days. It was just about playing and challenging ourselves to be better. We were both learning at the same time.

At one time in Brian's golf days, he played in the same tournaments as Kevin Na. Kevin Na was suspended for a year from the Southern California Junior Golf Association for an encounter with a club pro that caused a suspension. While at that tournament, we didn't see what happened in the incident. This one-year suspension would drive Kevin to work tirelessly on his short and overall games. His work ethic was incredible, and he probably made a giant step in conquering the 10,000-hour rule for mastery of his skill during that year of suspension. I don't doubt that this is what happened.

After being reinstated, Kevin was a very successful junior player. Na was a two-time Rolex Junior All-American who competed in the American Junior Golf Association from 1997-2001. Although he won just two tournaments, he finished second several times, including in the 2001 Rolex Tournament of Champions. He quickly turned pro after his junior year in high school in 2000 at seventeen. He won the Volvo Masters of Asia in South Korea in 2002. His career took off from there. Undoubtedly, his mother and father were instrumental in his success. Both Jung Hye-won and Yong Na made sacrifices that most will never know.

Kevin won on the PGA Tour five times. He also won other tournaments in Korea and tours in the United States. Kevin has been as tenacious about doing well in golf as any player one might see today. Despite injuries over his career, he has done quite well. During his career, he has conquered many challenges, one of which was his swing. At one point, he was afraid of pulling the trigger and swinging the golf club. He tenaciously fought the demons in his head about this problem and conquered it. It took a lot of courage to overcome that. He has lasted a long time on the tour, and it was just sheer determination that allowed him to continue to keep his PGA Tour card. He has made a magnificent living playing golf, but rest assured, it was not easy.

Kevin Na is one of the unusual success stories from the same era as Brian. Kevin did not even finish high school much less go to college or play the amateur tour much before turning pro. It was high risk, but he had a fundamental tool in his bag that many of the players we will encounter in this narrative did not have: his putting. He was always a great putter. I saw that when he was a young player, and he used it to do quite well despite all the hazards put in front of him.

Although I don't know what Kevin did to conquer his swing issue, he gutted it out. He has since resigned from the PGA Tour and has joined LIV Golf, a story for another time. What is important is that he was one of the first players from the same era as Brian who was highly motivated to become a PGA Tour player.

There are so many factors that come into play before one can arrive at that level. Having the sheer determination to make it is one of those factors. He set a goal to get to the PGA Tour and did what he had to do to make it. One of my teaching pros said that sheer guts is needed to get there. Even though this narrative is not about how to get to the PGA Tour, all the players in this story who were from the same era as Brian had that as their goal. They all wanted to play on the PGA Tour. They were all reaching for the "Golden Ring." Except my son.

I taught Brian how to hit balls starting at the age of seven, but he had worked with the short game and putting for a long time before hitting golf balls. He had an area where we could chip and putt at the house, and he did a great deal of it there. Watching his putting was a thing to behold because he could sink them from anywhere. He had no fear when he was putting on a golf ball. More importantly, he had a gift for it. After watching hundreds of players over the last fifty years of observing golf, I know some are better at putting than others. They have the gift of touch, the ability to feel the putt that needs to be made. We have all seen the magic of Jack Nicklaus at essential moments in his career and the great Tiger Woods: both had exceptional putting skills not just honed by practice, but also a genetic gift given to them that allowed them to perform at the highest levels of golf. If there is anything that separates the top-level player from the rest of those who play this great game, it is putting that makes the difference. If a player is putting well, they are at the top of the leaderboard; if they are not, they are slamming the trunk and moving on to the next tournament.

Brian had that gift; otherwise, he would not have been able to accomplish the things he did in golf as a Junior Amateur.

Chapter 3: 1990

Jack Nicklaus/Chris Tidland/Phil Mickelson, and Joining a Country Club

"Resolve never to quit, never to give
up, no matter the situation."

Jack Nicklaus

Because we could see that Brian was quite comfortable with a golf club in his hands at nine years old, we decided to join a country club. A new club had made an enticing offer to participate in its initial year, Dove Canyon Country Club in Coto de Caza, CA. It was a Jack Nicklaus golf course, and it was a beauty. If one does not have room in the backyard for a green and a sand trap, then the best alternative is to join a country club. Entering the country club was an absolute joy, and we could not wait to get out there and play the course. We played there at every opportunity we had. The opportunity to play at a country club is what allowed Brian to grow.

Brian took to playing the course as if he owned it. We had played the Newport Beach Golf Course on Irvine Avenue many times before we joined Dove Canyon, so it was easy for him to adjust to playing at the new club. He was pretty successful right away, and he broke 80 from the red tees when he was still nine years old. The course was 5225 yards from those tees and a par 72. The Newport Beach Golf Course was only 3216 yards and a par 59.

One of the great benefits of playing Dove Canyon was the rugged design by Nicklaus. There were design elements in the golf course of his experience playing golf in Scotland that had a bit of "unfairness." If one hit the green, the ball had better stay in one area because an off-center hit might catch one of the drop-offs from the green that left the player in trouble. The next shot required a good shot to get up and down for par. The Nicklaus course taught us more about how to handle shots like that and improved our short game. As was always the case with Brian, getting on the green was just a putt away from par or birdie.

Jack Nicklaus came to Dove Canyon Country Club to dedicate the course by playing an inaugural round (as he had done with all the 400 courses he built). During that inaugural round, Jack found himself stuck about thirty yards right behind a tree on the left side of the fairway of a par 5. The club members were able to follow Jack around as he played the inaugural round with Angel baseball player Wally Joyner on November 19, 1991. Since we members could follow the players closely on the fairway, I was within earshot of Jack and asked, "Who put that tree there?" Everyone who heard the comment laughed, and Jack said, "What tree?" With 250 yards of distance to cover the green, Jack pulled out a five-wood and lined himself up to hit the ball through the "Y" in the tree! He set up, turned, and fired. Right through the tree the ball sailed up in the air and landed about 2 yards off the green to the right of the pin! Nicklaus then chipped the ball to within a foot of the hole and birdied it. He demonstrated to us why he was the great Jack Nicklaus.

At the end of the round, Jack Nicklaus came off the green on the 18th hole, said hello to Brian, and said, "I hear you are a pretty good player. Well, keep it up, and good luck with your golf." Brian was so thrilled to meet the great Jack Nicklaus that when we went back to the clubhouse, I told Brian to take something to Mr. Nicklaus and have his autograph on it. Brain found three things to autograph running back and forth to get them before he finished because I told him to stop bugging the poor man. Jack Nicklaus was not phased. He signed all three items for Brian. When Mr. Nicklaus was leaving, I nodded to him and said thank you for being so wonderful to Brian. He said, "He's a great kid." And off Jack went to the waiting helicopter that flew him directly to the airport. In 1991, Jack Nicklaus was still a big deal. It would be the only time we met him but watching him golf that day was just a pleasure.

During his time at Dove Canyon Country Club, I invited a former student to play golf with us. His name was Chris Tidland. Chris was in my English class as a sophomore at Valencia High School in Placentia, CA, and I learned he was quite a good golfer. I remember that his feet barely touched the floor when he was in class as he sat at his desk. Chris was a quiet, intelligent, and fun guy to have in class. He always did his work on time and never complained or caused an ounce of trouble, the kind of student all teachers like. By the end of his senior year, Chris had won the Southern California

High School Championship at Canyon Country Club, the same venue Brian would play at when he got to high school. I understand that his grandfather led Chris to love the game, mentored him as a young player, and got him to many of his tournaments. He crafted his game at Alta Vista Country Club in Placentia, and Hunter Mahan began his junior golf career at the same venue.

Chris went to Oklahoma State and won the NCAA Championship in 1995, taking down a tough Stanford team led by Tiger Woods. Chris turned pro in 1996 and played on the Nationwide and Canadian Tours for several years. He went to PGA "Q" School (Qualifying School) thirteen times and got his card several times but was unable to hold onto it. Chris resolved never to quit and would not have done so had it not been for family. He continued to play on the mini tours until shoulder surgery altered his swing mechanics, and he struggled after that.

Chris was a winner on the Nationwide Tour a couple of times and qualified for the U.S. Open four or five times, only cutting once. If there was ever a guy who gave it his all to be a permanent player on the PGA Tour, it was Chris Tidland. He is currently the head pro at Stillwater Country Club in Stillwater, Oklahoma, where he resides with his wife and two adult children.

The day that Chris came to play golf with Brian and me was a real treat. Brian was exposed to a good golf professional and how he conducted himself around the golf course. It was a treat for Chris to play at Dove Canyon because he encountered plenty of Nicklaus courses as a player.

I had Chris in his cart and at the first hole, I told Chris that Brian would not play a Titleist golf ball. Chris asked why not, and I said, "I don't know, but he has it in his head that playing that ball will not do him well." Chris turned and saw Brian on the fairway about to hit his next shot and yelled over to him, "Brian, don't you know that Titleist golf balls are the best you can play?" Brian was unmoved and didn't reply. I suppose he knew I had put Chris up to saying something to him about the ball he was playing. It didn't matter because it would be a long while before Brian changed to playing the Titleist golf ball. It was an issue in his personality, a crack, an invisible problem that would come about over the next several years. My wife was already reading books like *How to Deal with a Stubborn Child*.

We went around the golf course playing and watching Chris rip gigantic drive after drive and show Brian how to approach hitting the next shot. He was so professional and so friendly to Brian. Now one might think that I would be saying to Brian later that this is what it is like to be a PGA Tour player, but the whole experience was not about that, and I never intended it to be. It was just about how one conducts oneself on the golf course like a pro, like a good golfer. We both learned a lot from Chris and had a wonderful time. We would see him one more time at the Independent Insurance Agents Junior Golf Tournament, the third-oldest junior golf tournament in the country. Juniors play with touring pros in that tournament to let them see what it is like to play with a professional golfer. Brian qualified for the National Tournament and went to Indiana to play, and that is where we saw Chris again. While Chris Tidland may not be a household name to golfers, he made a Herculean effort to become a permanent pro on the tour.

One day in the summer of 1990, Brian and I were playing a round at the Dove Canyon Country Club when the club professional came up and told us that Phil Mickelson was playing in front of us. We tried to play fast enough to see him hit his tee shots, but we only managed to see a couple on the front side. When we got to the turn, we had to stop at the halfway house because their burger and fries were superb. There Phil was, sitting with his playing buddy, eating one of our choice hamburgers. I told Brian to get his autograph, and he did. Phil was cheerful and delighted to sign a scorecard and probably never realized it would be one of his notable characteristics as a player: Phil signed enormous numbers of autographs. He endeared himself to his fans for doing so.

Phil became one of golf's great players. When meeting him in the summer of 1990, he had won the NCAA Divison I golf championship in both his first and second years in college. He would win again in his senior year and become a three-time Jack Nicklaus Player of the Year, three-time Haskins Player of the Year, win sixteen individual titles, and a four-time First Team Ping All-American. Pretty impressive college career to say the least. It is just amazing who one meets when playing a game of golf.

Although this was our first year at Dove Canyon, that summer would be the first time I would enter Brian into a playing competition. He was already beating me with his scores from the Red Tees at Dove Canyon. The club owner, Garth Chambers, took Brian out for a round of golf and just could not believe how good he was. Brian made a seven-foot putt on the last hole, and Garth just shook his head and said, "Dad, he's a great player and a great kid." I thought so, too.

Chapter 4: 1991

Hunter Mahan and Winning
the First Tournament

"When I see you out on the golf course all the time
with your son, I am amazed at your dedication to
him. It is incredibly gratifying to see that, and I
just want you to know how I view your effort."

Newport Beach Member

Since Brian had the opportunity to play at Dove Canyon
Country Club from eight years old until about eleven, it was
quite helpful to all aspects of his game. The practice facilities
at this club were stellar, and it was a foundation builder to be
able to practice out of great bunkers and great chipping greens
to increase the practice time. After that, he would play at
Newport Beach Country Club, which was much closer to our
home. Playing at Newport allowed him to get to the course,

practice, and come home relatively quickly. The only issue with Newport at the time was that there wasn't a good place to practice hitting out of the sand. It took practicing sand shots on the golf course to learn effective techniques. However, the greens were quite good, and the putting facility was excellent.

The club began supporting the Champions Tour starting in 1995. It was called the Hoag Classic. The benefit to the membership was the improved conditioning of the golf course. It was in excellent shape for the Hoag Classic and then for the membership for several weeks after the match. For Brian, joining a country club nearby benefited his game and his inspiration. I would play hundreds of rounds with him while he grew up there. We also would meet some nice people over the period of time they held the golf tournament. Most of the best players on the PGA Tour who had turned fifty were now playing on the PGA Senior Tour.

In the summer of 1991, Brian was just nine years old, but he competed in the Southern California Junior Golf Association in the eleven and underage group. The eleven and under group played from the Red Tees or the lady's tees in each tournament. The organization contacted private country clubs and public golf courses to determine who would be willing to give up one day of the golf course for all players. The other age groups in the organization were 12-13, 14-15, and 16-18. These age demarcations were for boys and girls, and they played on the same golf course but at different times. The boys all teed off first, and then the girl groups. The players came from all over Southern California to compete in these junior tournaments.

Four players in Brian's age group dominated the eleven and underage group: Brian Sinay, James Oh, Steve Conway, and Hunter Mahan. The first three were all the same age, but Hunter was one year younger than the other three but always competed well against the other three. Playing successful golf as a very young player indicates that the player has a future in the game perhaps but not necessarily at the professional level. Different factors will come into play to determine the "flame out" age of all these players. It just happens at different times. James Oh was the premier player at the time, but the victories in junior golf tournaments around Southern California were shared by the three players, as mentioned above. Hunter was almost always fourth. After a significant junior tournament, Hunter had finished 4th behind the three greedy winners, James, Brian, and Steve. I told Hunter, "You keep working on that short game, and you will find yourself winning down the road." I said it to be nice, and because he was such a great kid. Before long, Hunter's dad, Monte Hunter, the central figure behind the development of Hunter' game, decided to move to Texas and take his son Hunter to get instructed by Hank Haney. I had heard of Hank Haney as a golf instructor and his connection with Mark O'Meara. Monte was determined to make Hunter a good golfer, so he sold his California house and used the money to get the very best instruction for Hunter. He was one of those parents determined to make his son a player on the PGA Tour. It just goes to show how much parents support the goal of their aspiring golfers. It was a big gamble, given that Hunter had three players beating him in the Southern California region. But Monte was brighter than the other three dads. He gave him an instructor that would give him a winning golf swing. I assumed that Hunter wanted the same thing as he went along with the move and received high-level instruction from the teacher of Mark O'Meara and, eventually, Tiger Woods. It paid off.

At Aronimink Golf Course, where Brian qualified for the 1997 U.S. Junior Amateur, we reconnected with our friends by running into Hunter Mahan and his father, Monte. Monte told me Hunter was trying to get his club to a specific position at the top. He was speaking a language with which I was unfamiliar, and I knew that it would not be long before Hunter passed up Brian.

Hunter would win the 1999 5A Texas State High School Golf Championship and the 1999 U.S. Junior Amateur besting fellow Texan Matthew Rosenfeld. Hunter's skills had improved dramatically after working with Hank Haney. As some readers may know, Hunter became an All-American at Oklahoma State and then had an outstanding PGA Tour career, including playing for the Ryder Cup team. He won on the PGA Tour six times, including a World Golf Championship, a challenging tournament with the best players on the PGA Tour participating. Hunter was in the top ten in all the majors, and with just a break or two here and there, he would have been a significant winner in the majors. He was ranked as high as fourth in the world at one time, another highly admirable accomplishment.

I believe Hunter became a better player when he got outstanding instruction from Hank Haney. But instruction is not the only thing. A good player must be an excellent putter, and Hunter was always that.

It was gratifying to see how well he succeeded. He was a great kid when he played with Brian as a young golfer. Hunter had wanted to be a PGA Tour player, and he got there. He grabbed onto the "Golden Ring" and held it for quite a while.

At nine, Brian won his first tournament in Borrego Springs, CA, east of San Diego, on a windy day. Parents were allowed to follow along if they wished and watch the players. I did.

The tournaments for the eleven and under group in those days were just nine holes. The lowest score wins the trophy. Brian shot a 42 in a hellacious wind and took first place. It would be the first of many at these local tournaments that he would win. Although the drive out to that region east of San Diego was long and winding down a valley into a very difficult sun. The drive home was much easier as Brian held onto his first trophy. It was a challenging but fun day.

Later in the summer, Brian played in the famous Yorba Linda Junior Invitational, a tournament that drew all the best players from Southern California because the trophies were so big, and the country club treated the players like royalty. The head pro was Tom Sargeant, who would eventually be Brian's first professional teacher. He ran a great tournament, and Brian participated in it as a nine-year-old and missed the cut after the first day by one stroke. It was a good showing with so many good players a year or so older than him. A player has to be eleven through the end of the tournament but can turn twelve the following day and still be eligible for the eleven and under category. Brian was not daunted by the competition but was energized by it.

Chapter 5: 1992

J. J. Killeen/Matthew Rosenfeld/ Lorena Ochoa and The Japan Cup

"Just try to be the best you can be; never cease trying
to be the best you can be. That's in your power."

John Wooden

The San Diego Junior World Championship is the world's biggest and most challenging junior golf tournament. The event attracted 475 junior golfers from seven countries and 20 states in its inaugural year. Today, the tournament has grown to 1250 participants, representing 56 countries and 42 states. The IMG Academy Junior World Golf Championships is now the most significant international event in the world and is unique for its international representation and cultural diversity. My son, Brian, started playing in the tournament when he was ten. In those days, the ten and under category meant that even an eight-year-old could compete against the ten-year-old. A few years before, in 1985, Tiger Woods competed as an eight-year-old and won his first Junior World Title. He would end up with six of them, a record.

The year 1992 saw his entrance into that tournament by Brian at the age of ten. The course he played was at the Presidio Golf Course in Old Town, San Diego. The tiny course is only 1254 yards long with nine par 3's on the front, and nine par 3's on the back. Most holes are short and require a delicate touch to get onto the greens, which are relatively small and difficult to manage. The course is a par 54 with a 27 score on the front and 27 on the back. One can stand at one point near the small clubhouse and see all eighteen holes. It is an enjoyable miniature golf course. Some of my fond remembrances of this course were the times my son and I went down to play the course before the tournament. The tournament took place sometime in July, so we had to fit in some practice rounds to learn the nuances of the course before the tournament.

Whenever we visited the golf course, Brian would play it several times. We went there about five times before he felt ready to play in the tournament. The best thing about going down there was the Old Town Mexican Cafe, a Mexican eatery that has been there since 1977. Brian played the course enough to say he was ready for the tournament, and it was not long before the first day arrived. There were about fifty players on the field from all over the world and the country. This tournament was a big one, and it was a big deal.

At the end of the third round, Brian scored 161, or one under par for the three days. The tournament winner was one of his buddies from the Southern California region named James Oh. He shot a total of 157, or 5 under par. They were the only two to shoot under par on the golf course for the three-day tournament. It is, however, the Junior World Title that gives distinction. Often this tournament victory is mentioned as a significant amateur career victory.

As parents, we were amazed and happy to see Brian succeed at such a high level. The massive benefit of finishing in second, and those boys and girls in all five divisions who finished in 6th place, is that they received an all-expenses trip to Japan to play in The Japan Cup if they wanted to go. We had to stay for a couple more hours to complete paperwork for the trip to Japan in two weeks. We found out that this would be the second year of the tournament in Japan. It was sponsored by the Chubu Nippon Broadcasting Company, making the Japan Cup Junior Golf Championships a reality. They played the match in Kani City, Japan, on August 28, 29, and 30th at the Fuji Syuga Country Club.

There were four levels of players: ages 10 and under, ages 11-12; ages 13-14; and ages 15-17. There would be twenty-four male and twenty-four female players from the Junior World International Tournament and an equal number of players from Japan who would qualify for The Japan Cup before the International players arrived. What made this special was that they filmed the entire tournament for Japanese TV, which would be shown as a junior tournament in Japan in the fall of that year. We were sent a copy of the TV program to watch on our TVs, but the whole thing was in Japanese and a bit difficult to follow. Nonetheless, it promised to be a great experience.

The players who went on the trip were greeted at the airport with considerable fanfare and then driven to Nagoya to stay at a five-star hotel called Hotel Nagoya. It was just spectacular, and the following day, I took the players and their parents to the golf course for a practice round of golf. At the end of the practice round, the entire group was treated to a welcoming party put on by the tournament's sponsors. The other sponsors of the tournament were major Japanese corporations like Toyota, Sony, Hitachi, Mizuno, Honda, Panasonic, and several others. The CEO of the Chubu Nippon Broadcasting Company, Mr. Kazuo Takahashi, gave a welcoming speech, congratulated the players for doing so well in the San Diego Junior World Tournament, and wished them luck playing here in Japan in the tournament called The Japan Cup. The players and family then helped themselves to incredibly wonderful hors d'oeuvres and drinks and sushi (if one so desired). The players were taken back to the hotel, and they just had a wonderful time acting like little brats in the hotel.

The following day we went down to the dining room for breakfast, which was a sumptuous affair. The food was all American with eggs, bacon, sausages, orange juice, and Danish pastry. We ate our first breakfast in Japan and could not believe how wonderful it was. Everyone had to be ready by a particular time to get on the bus, take the one-hour drive out to the golf course owned by the corporations, and play the first round of golf. When we got on the bus, our tour guide walked on and said, "Ohayo...." Well, in Japanese, it meant good morning. After she said that, I commented, "I'm from California, not Ohio." Well, at her expense, the entire bus cracked up, but it was all great fun.

The primary issue at Fuji Syuga Country Club was that it was complicated to walk because the course was quite hilly, and it was being held in the middle of August when Japan was hot and humid. It was fun but challenging. The first round was in the books and Brian was near the top of the leaderboard. His Japanese opponents were good players but were at a different level than the American or International players who also made it to Japan. At the end of the tournament, Brian found himself in third place, a few strokes behind James Oh, his childhood nemesis, and his friend Travis Whisman. It was a great tournament, and the final ceremony was just spectacular as only the Japanese can do.

The end of the tournament celebration was just as spectacular as the welcoming party. There were giant Japanese drums beat with timed regularity like a war dance. Ladies in Japanese apparel danced and twirled batons, and fans feathered their faces. The drinks were plentiful and the food sumptuous, and another major CEO made another speech about one of the sponsoring companies. He said in Japanese but translated for us, "Golf is like life. There are good times, and there are bad times. The measure of the person is how they address the bad times. Whether they pick themselves up and get back into the competition after a mistake or two." I heard that message clearly, but I am not sure my mini-me listened to the same thing.

On this trip, we sat near a young lady and her mother on their way to the same golf tournament. We were not aware of the results of the girl's game at Junior World. In any case, the young lady's name was Lorena Ochoa, a player from Guadalajara, Mexico, who had won first place as a ten-year-old. She would go on to win the tournament in Japan by ten strokes at 25 under par and dominated the field. Here was a young lady who intended to become an LPGA player. She was motivated and wanted to do so when she could swing a golf club. She had a marvelous smile and a wonderful personality. We sat and talked to her on the long plane ride from Los Angeles to Japan. Since my wife could speak Spanish, she managed to converse with Lorena and her mother in English and Spanish.

Lorena was good right from the get-go at age ten, and she was naturally gifted, but there would still be a lot of hard work before she managed to get to the tour. There were often comparisons between her and Tiger Woods because she was so good at such a young age. Despite an outstanding collegiate career, she doubted that she could do well in the Ladies Professional Golf Association. Her doubts were quickly wiped out by her excellent performances in her first year on tour. How is it so easy for some and so difficult for others? During her junior career, wherever we went, Lorena's mother, Marcela Reyes, was there by her side supporting her efforts.

Lorena would become one the best players in the LPGA, who held the number one position in lady's golf for 158 weeks or nearly three years, a record that stands today. She won thirty times in ten years as a professional, twenty-seven LPGA titles, and two majors.

She retired at age twenty-eight to raise a family. She was one of those people who was easy to predict as a future successful golfer. She never ceased to try to be the best that she could be. Sometimes people from the outside see it better than the player themselves since golf is such a fickle game. It is fickle for one round and inconsistent for one's entire career. Sometimes one break makes a difference in whether a player succeeds or fails. Ask Tom Lehman.

Two other players that performed in this tournament were J. J Killeen from San Diego and Matthew Rosenfeld from Dallas, Texas. Matthew was a year younger than Brian, so in the ten and under the group. Matthew would finish ninth. The following year he would win the tournament as a ten-year-old and thus began his journey to be a pro. Eventually, he would win the 2000 U.S. Junior Amateur at Pumpkin Ridge Golf Club in North Plains, Oregon. He was just the sixth stroke-play medalist in championship history. By the end of that year, he was also the American Junior Golf Association's Player of the Year.

Matthew had an outstanding Junior Amateur career. He had

an up-and-down career in college for the Texas Longhorns, yet he managed to win the Conference championship in his senior year. Matthew struggled with his swing in college, and perhaps switching teachers a lot managed to get into his head too much, but that is what I just read about him. After college, he did not qualify for the Nationwide Tour, so he played Monday qualifiers, and despite playing well, his scores always fell a bit short. When he did allow it, he made enough money to be even at the end of the day. He tried the Asian tour for two years and played well, but when he played poorly in 2012, he was out of money. He was twenty-nine, and he couldn't envision himself as a guy still chasing his PGA Tour dreams anymore. When we were in Japan together, we had the best of times. Matthew's father, Mike, was just a super fun guy who did all he could to support Matthew's efforts.

Another player who was always right there when the results of Junior World were tallied was J. J. Killeen from San Diego, CA. He was fourth when Brian was second at age ten; he was second to Brian at age twelve. He was a young, dedicated player who also intended to become a PGA Tour player.

He played college golf at Texas Christian University and turned professional in 2005. Killeen played on mini tours, including the Tight Lies Tour and the NGA Hooters Tour, before joining the Nationwide Tour in 2008. Killeen won his first Nationwide Tour event in 2011 at the Utah Championship and again at the Cox Classic in Nebraska the following week. Killeen ended the 2011 season as the top money earner on the Nationwide Tour, which granted him a full-season exemption on the PGA Tour for 2012. He was voted the Nationwide Tour Player of the year in 2012. For the last several years, J.J has played at various times on different mini tours. The ever and consistent support of his mother, Suze, and father, Joe, was always apparent when anyone saw J.J. play. He is still knocking on the door of professional golf, still looking to grab hold of that "Golden Ring."

Aside from the Junior World tournament, Brain played in tournaments sponsored by the Southern California Junior Golf Association. Players competed against each other by signing up for the tournament and showing up for the one-day tournament. Sometimes the club would hold a two-day tournament as Yorba Linda Country Club did in those days.

As a ten-year-old, Brian won about ten local tournaments in the Southern California Junior Golf Association. He was consistently in the top five over his year as a ten-year-old. Suffice it to say that it was a good year, with the cap being the second-place finish at the Junior World Tournament. He also shot even par from the red tees at Dove Canyon Country Club. He had a good start on his way to Stanford, though he didn't know about that school at that age and wouldn't learn about it for a couple more years when he devoted himself to attending the school on a golf scholarship. At age ten, he was considered in the top five in the 11 and under category in Southern California, a pretty big area with plenty of competition.

Chapter 6: 1993

James Oh and Junior World

"Setting goals is the first step in turning
the invisible into the visible."

Tony Robbins

Brian had a lot of golf successes in 1993. Junior World took place at the Pine Glen Golf Course at Singing Hills in El Cajon, CA, a three-course public golf establishment where the boys and girls aged 11-12 played their championship. This course was a bit larger than the last one with 2508 yards, eighteen holes, and each of them par 3's. It was a par 54 golf course. There were two-hundred-yard par 3 holes and a 184-yard par 3. The Pine Glenn course was pretty challenging for an eleven-year-old. We took the time to play the course before the golf tournament about six different times. This course was an hour and a half away from our home in Irvine, so we made the trips on Saturdays to get into the necessary practice and learn the nuances of the course.

The dedication was worth it because Brian finished third in the tournament with a score of 165, or just three over par. The winner was Michael Hastings from Washington, but some other notable players in the field are of interest. In sixth place was Joe Skovron of Murrieta, with a score of 168. Who is Joe Skovron? Some readers might recognize him from the PGA Tour as the caddie for Ricky Fowler. Joe has been the only caddie for Ricky since Ricky turned pro. They became friends in junior golf, and when it came time to choose a caddie, Joe was Ricky's choice. Joe was an excellent junior golfer and an outstanding high school player in Murrieta at the same high school that Ricky attended.

Another player in the tournament was Dusty Schmidt, a Southern California Junior Golf Association player who played in many matches with Brian. Dusty eventually became good friends with Kevin Na and shared some great times. Dusty was well known as the player who walked fast to his ball and hit before other players behind him could hit.

The most notable player in the field was the winner of the previous year's tournament, James Oh. He could only manage fifteenth in the tournament with a score of 172. Again, this was just one tournament, which does not mean that Brian was better than James. It happens all the time on the PGA Tour. Great players do not always finish first. It is the total of their playing that marks the level of the player. James and his dad always had goals in front of them. Mike talked about them.

When James Oh came onto the junior golf circuit, he was just a tiny guy, but he had golf skills. His father was a teaching pro, but because he didn't speak a lot of English, I could never verify that with him. It did not affect James' future performance in junior tournaments because James finished his junior career with significant results. James won the U.S Junior

Amateur at Conway Farms CC in Forest, Illinois. He defeated Aaron Baddeley, a highly successful player on the PGA Tour. In the first two qualifying rounds for this junior amateur, Brian played with Aaron Baddeley in what would be challenging winds. I remember that Brian got down on his knees and bowed to Aaron after the second round of golf because Aaron had shot excellent scores in the brutal, challenging winds. It was beneficial to be a player from Australia. Aaron knew how to hit a knockdown shot like a pro at that age.

Aaron was ranked number one after the first two rounds, which qualified for the top 64 for match play. The two days saw terrible winds for the players, so Brian was eligible with a 79-71. Aaron shot in the 60s both days, the only one to do so. Aaron's performance taught me that Aaron had better instruction than Brian because he knew how to deal with the wind. The wind did not die out until all the players had finished. James Oh would beat Aaron in the final and win the Junior Amateur.

James also had other significant accomplishments as a junior player. James won the 1998 Southern California High School Championship in high school, a notable achievement. Although he won this tournament only once, he competed in the other three high school championships.

James also won the American Junior Golf Association Tournament of Champions twice, matching only the great Phil Mickelson in that feat. His amateur career was concise because he turned pro after one year of college at the University of Nevada in Las Vegas. He turned pro in 2001. James, however, only won one professional tournament, and that was on the Nationwide Tour. While he qualified for the PGA Tour in Q school, he needed to earn more money to keep his tour card and never recovered after 2009. James had tried to make it on the PGA Tour for ten years but was never able to do so. He hit the ball too short on his drives because of his size and was not a great putter. He did not have that great touch necessary for a PGA Tour player. I am only guessing from the vast experience I had watching him play. I felt that Brian had a much better putting stroke than James, but that is a Dad's opinion.

Today James Oh is considered one of the best short-game teachers in the country, with several pros going to him for instruction. He has managed to send several players to college with scholarships because of his teaching. He had that to fall back on as a career because he was on the fast track to becoming a PGA Tour pro. Going this route could be better.

Winning was an opportunity to go to Japan on an all-expense paid trip. It was the same experience the year early, with a three-day tournament and hospitality from the Japanese. In the end, Brian finished in the top ten against twelve-year-olds. During the summer of 1993, Brian won at least ten Southern California Junior Golf Association tournaments and remained a top-five player in Southern California.

Chapter 7: 1994

Steve Conway and The Stanford Story

"People don't seem to realize how often you have
to come in second to finish first. I've never met a
winner who hadn't learned how to be a loser."

Jack Nicklaus

Brian played in the San Diego Junior World Golf tournament for the third year in a row in 1994 and had a stellar year. Again, the 11-12 division played at the same Pine Glen Golf Course at Singing Hills. It was the same course as last year but less daunting, given that he had grown some more. Brian played three spectacular rounds of golf and finished in the first place. He could now call himself a Junior World Champion; he was just five championships short of Tiger Woods. He finished in first place with a two-over-par score of 164 and just ahead of three future pro golfers: JJ Killeen, Travis Whisman, and James Oh.

Brian had gone head-to-head with James in the final round as James had a one-stroke lead.

Because the course was so small, it could not accommodate parents to watch their players on the course, so it was a waiting game. All the players had come in, and only James and Brian were the last to finish out the field. They went to the last hole, a 100-yard par 3 with a small green and an area where all the people gathered around and were able to watch the final hole of play. I did not know how Brian was doing, but I thought it was a good sign when he hit first off the tee on number eighteen. He also had great confidence when he hit his ball to the green, and it landed and stuck 10 feet from the pin. Huge applause came from the crowd. Then James Oh hit his shot and hit the green. Again, massive applause for the players and one of which would probably be the champion. As Brian walked down the fairway with great assurance, I felt he had done well. He got to the green, fixed his ball mark, looked over at me, and said without any sound coming out of his mouth, "I won." Coming in second two years earlier had taught Brian the value of striving to win.

I was in disbelief because Brian had beaten the great James Oh head-to-head. Brian then lined up his putt and narrowly missed it but tapped it in for a three. Then James Oh did the same, and the golf tournament was over. Brian Sinay was a Junior World Champion, something that few people can claim. A little-known fact is that Phil Mickelson won Junior World just once, at the age of ten. A lot of good pros were Junior World Champions like Lorena Ochoa, Tiger Woods, Craig Stadler, Corey Pavin, Pat Perez, David Toms, Amy Alcott, Brandie Burton, and Notah Begay, among others. I recalled a quote by Jack Nicklaus, "People don't seem to know how often you have to come in second in order to finish first. I never met a winner who hadn't learned how to be a loser."

I remember calling my wife to tell her Brian had won and that it would be a while before we got home because we had to do the ceremony and fill out the papers for another trip to Japan. I was delighted and so happy for this young man who had worked hard on his game and got ready to play again. Brian beat 154 players from all over the world and became a Junior World Champion. Still, because of this victory, he had no intention of becoming a pro. It did not change his mind set about golf; it was just golf, and he had no ulterior motive.

Steve Conway, who lived in Irvine near us, had participated in the junior tournaments with Brian in Southern California. He was a good player and loved golf. He had an admirable career as a player for the University of California at Los Angles but could not make it to the PGA Tour.

Steve would go to the tournaments with us during the summer because his dad worked full time, and the mother had another younger child to take care of. His mother was also always there to get Steve to his junior tournaments. Both parents were highly supportive. Steve was a great kid who loved golf more than Brian. He would read books and magazines, and his life was filled with the sport of golf. Whenever the two of them would get together, they played golf video games or chipped Wiffle balls around the house and tried to make different shots. They enjoyed each other's company. They had a lot of fun together and were a good match for one another. Around the summer, Steve was visiting the house, and he started a conversation with Brian about where his dad went to college. "Stanford," Steve told Brian. "Where is that?" asked Brian. And the conversation went on about the college, and the result was that Brian decided he wanted to go there. Not long after that, he wore a Stanford sweatshirt; he wore it to school a lot in the sixth grade.

Not long after Brian won the San Diego Junior World title, I asked him to send a letter to Wally Goodwin, the coach of Stanford. It was the same approach that Tiger Woods took when he was in the seventh grade and asked Wally if he could play golf for him at Stanford. It was not long after that when Wally showed up at a golf tournament that Brian was playing in, introduced himself to me, and thus began his following of Brian throughout the next five or so years.

Wally Goodwin was a nice guy. He was a Tommy Lasorda guy full of rah-rah and encouraging speech. Thus began the journey for Brian to win a scholarship to Stanford and play where Tiger Woods and Tom Watson played. He grabbed onto that idea like a bulldog and never let it go until he had accomplished it. For once, Brian Sinay had a purpose for his golf: get a scholarship to Stanford. There was no mention of playing for the PGA.

Certainly, one of the things that helped Brian was that he was on the right academic track. He was an outstanding student in elementary school, as was his sister Jennie who modeled good academic skills two years ahead of Brian. One of our decisions was to make both kids the "older" students in the class. A Harvard-Yale study concluded after twenty years that students who are the oldest in the class get eighty percent of the academic and athletic scholarships. It was recommended that it would be wise to make them older in their classes than the youngest. Therefore, we "held them back," and they both entered kindergarten about as old as they could be as one was already six (Brian), and one would be six in October (Jennie). Although they were twenty-two months apart, they were two grades apart in school. They both excelled in elementary school. Parents were becoming aware of the advantage of being the oldest in the class.

Both children then had an additional year of reading before they got to kindergarten. Brian would eventually issue a "complaint" to the administration of his elementary school for him being admonished for wanting to read in kindergarten. His kindergarten teacher scolded him for doing so. It reminded me of Scout's problem with her elementary teacher in To Kill a Mockingbird when she was not allowed to read. Atticus, her father, had to devise a compromise to alleviate the upset Scout for not being able to read in elementary school. Brain waited until he made his sixth-grade graduation speech to send chills to the faculty member who scolded him for doing so. This ability to read early and read well was a massive advantage for both kids. Academically, they both did very well in elementary school, junior high school, and high school. They were both nearly straight-A students by the time they finished high school. This did not mean that their schooling was accessible because they attended one of the most challenging, if not the most difficult, high school in Orange County, CA. University High School in Irvine is recognized as one of California's leading academic public high schools. It is said that they graduate as many as ten students to Stanford each year. In any case, it was a school that prepared students for college and complex academic challenges.

That August, we went to Japan for the third time, and it was a blast. This time we spent a lot of time with Matthew Rosenfeld and his dad, Mike. When it came to being tough on a kid, Mike was as tough as they get. He drove Matthew to succeed.

While Brian and Matthew ran around the hotel and had the Japanese administrators of the tournament pulling out their hair, Mike and I walked through the streets of Nagoya, looking for a place to eat. Along the way, on the streets, were vending machines where one could buy a cold beer. We got a tall beer and walked through the city looking for good food. We happened upon a restaurant that did not welcome us and turned us away. We were yelled at by patrons who still hated Americans because of Hiroshima and Nagasaki. We went elsewhere and found a small business where we sat, pointed, ordered food, drank the beers we brought, and had a wonderful time. It would be the last time we saw the Rosenfeld's as Matthew was two years behind Brian and would play in tournaments Brian was too old to play in anymore.

We were stupid dads just trying to push our kids to excel, and they did well despite our pushing. Yet, people have two views about this "pushing": if one doesn't, the kid does not try hard; if one does, the chances of success are more significant. Tiger Woods is an example of that. His dad pushed him, and he was forced to work hard. He was told he had to work twice as hard as others. There is no doubt about Tiger being pushed. Other stories of Brian's era are legendary. Mike Oh was equally as tough on James, and it sometimes backfired as it did at the Junior World Tournament against Brian, and sometimes it worked out well. Hunter Mahan had pushing that was known about but not as prominent as others. Some players who weren't pushed made it on tour, so there is no answer. In a Vogue Magazine essay, Serena William said, "I got pushed hard by my parents." She felt she would not have been successful had she not been pushed. The reality is that some kids can take the push, and others cannot. If they can, they learn to fight the adversity of playing a game at the highest level. If they can't, they fail. Some kids just don't have any adversity quotient. One's adversity quotient is a score that measures the ability of a person to deal with adversities in their life. It is a person's ability to face situations, problems, and obstacles in life.

At the end of the summer, the Southern California Golf Association had an awards ceremony for the top players in each division. Brian had won the prestigious Junior World Tournament and received the Player of the Year Award for his outstanding national and local play. The Association invited Tiger Woods to come, make a speech, and hand out the awards to the players. It was quite an honor to be given a trophy by one of his favorite players. It was Tiger's senior year in high school when he came to make the presentations, and the word was already out that he would attend Stanford. The award was given to Brian, then a handshake, we snapped the pictures, and two parents were excessively proud of his accomplishments.

After the awards ceremony, Tiger walked down the hall with his girlfriend. Brian and I walked in the opposite direction. I said, "Good luck at Stanford." Tiger smiled, said, "Thank you," and walked by. Brian was now motivated to get to Stanford and say that he had gone where Tiger had gone to school. Tiger and Brian's names would come together several times before Brian reached Stanford.

Brian had a successful summer on the local circuit, with eight victories at different events. He had moved up to the White Tees at Newport Beach Country Club and shot just one over at age twelve. He continued to be a top-five player in Southern California.

Chapter 8: 1995

Gary Player and South Lake Middle School

"The more I practice, the luckier I get."

Gary Player

With very few opportunities at the national level for junior golf, most of the playing in 1995 was at the local level. We spent a lot of time attending as many tournaments as possible. Allowing players to perform in many tournaments makes them feel comfortable under the different kinds of pressure that a tournament is under. Brian probably played as many as twenty tournaments that year, beginning in the spring and ending in the fall. He won fifteen different tournaments during this season. He was playing very, very good golf. More tournaments left us less time to prepare for the Junior World tournament in July, and there was a learning curve there, just like every other golf course one plays.

Junior World, held in July as usual, and this time, the young players had a regulation course to play at Mission Trails Golf Course, a 6000-yard William Bell course where Phil Mickelson's best performance was a finish in fourth place. Learning this is one of the lessons of this memoir. It doesn't matter what the results of any tournament are because it's how the player continues to develop over time that ensures their success. Early success with golf often turns out to be the precursor for later success in golf, and it is just not guaranteed. Other factors come into play.

Brian's performance in the 1995 Junior World tournament at age thirteen was good but not great. He finished twenty-ninth in a field of 132, scoring 221 or just five over par. His childhood adversary, James Oh, finished second and retaliated for the loss to Brian as a twelve-year-old at the same tournament. Mission Trails was a much more challenging golf course with hazards that made playing difficult. One of the holes had a high-tension wire running across the fairway, and the player could hit it even if they hit a perfect shot. Unfortunately, it happened to Brian, and the professionals at the golf course did not set up the rule of a reload in case a player hit the wire. When Brian hit the wire, we could not find the ball, and eventually, he ended up with a triple bogey on the hole. It was in the last round of the tournament, and it took him out of contention for the top five. His score for the final round was 76, four over par. This performance as a thirteen-year-old versus fourteen year-olds was pretty good. It is amazing how one year affects the distance a player can hit a ball.

Tiger Woods said that he credited his mother for the hard work of taking him to the tournaments around Southern California because there was nothing fun about the driving one had to do for these tournaments. We left at five in the morning to get there for the beginning of the tournament in Calabasas. We also went to tournaments in East San Diego, which involved an hour and a half of driving one way. If there is a way to get your good golfer to Stanford, then it happens with a lot of hard work. The long hours waiting for the player to finish 18 holes and all the players to complete for one to know the tournament results will test almost anyone's patience. Imagine doing about twenty tournaments in a year. It's challenging to occupy all the time waiting and a commitment that many wouldn't want. And because they don't want to do it; it affects the player's performance.

During this time, I was not worried about Brian's golf swing. I was unaware of the sophistication of the golf swing, and I thought it was too early to worry about getting that kind of instruction. I did know that getting an education from recognized professional instructors was expensive, and it was not within the budget to do something like that. So, I paid lesser-known instructors to teach him the golf swing.

This big mistake was starting to show up in more significant tournament play. But when this happened, I was unaware of what could improve the golf swing to make it consistent. He ended up playing with a combination of different instructors and not a notable instructor who has put players on the map. Other players' fathers indicated that Brian's swing was too steep. It took some time to correct it, but his swing was never as sharp because I did not have the resources to pay the best instructors. Then again, this was not about making it to the pros, so what was the concern for having a perfect swing?

This year would mark the first year of the Toshiba Classic at Newport Beach Country Club. It was here that we saw a significant number of the best players who had "graduated" from the regular tour to the fifty and over Senior's Tour. Among those players who came each year to play was the ageless Gary Player. If one did not know his record as a golfer, it was a shame because he was a nine-time major winner with three British Open Championships, three Masters titles, two PGA Championships, and one U.S. Open victory. Gary has the fourth-highest total in golf history and tied with Ben Hogan with the most major tournament victories. He has a total of 160 wins worldwide!

Gary was a fanatic at caring for himself and worked at it daily. He was always fit as a fiddle. His work ethic was, in part, why he accomplished so much. I read about his daily physical fitness routine, which was just incredible. His work ethic for golf was equally impressive. Once, he told this story in his book *Bunker Play* where he hit sand shots over and over until he made three in a row and how he left his dinner party to go forward with dinner while he accomplished that goal.

He gave a clinic to the people of the Newport Beach Country Club and invited everyone to come down to Roger Dunn's Golf Shop in Santa Ana, where he would personally sign anything that they bought there that had his logo on it. Going there allowed us to meet one of the greatest players of all time, so Brian and I went to the golf store and bought his book *Bunker Play* for him to sign. Then he said that he had seen Brian's swing and said," It's a good swing." I think Brian was about twelve or thirteen at the time.

Gary talked about the physicality of a player and said that it was important that the player not build upper body strength too much because it would interfere with the golf swing. He looked at my body first before he said that. I was top-heavy at the time. Brian, he thought, would end up the same way, so he discouraged working out with weights to build up the upper body. He indicated that a thinner, wiry body is better for golf than a bulky one. He had his routine and how he played without worrying about the interference of a built-up upper body.

Mr. Player signed *Bunker Play*; it was the Bible of sand play. Brian and I read it religiously because Mr. Player won the Masters knowing more about how to get out of the sand than Arnold Palmer at the time of his 1961 Masters victory. He was a lovely man, gave us a reasonable amount of time, and we were so happy to meet him. I told Brian that I had better work harder at getting in shape. Reaching goals in golf has much to do with being in shape, and Gary Player was the first golfer to recognize that importance. And practicing hard was also one of his greatest assets.

Later on, that summer, Brian played at the Rolling Hills Country Club Junior Championship. There was an overall trophy for the best score of all the players. At age thirteen, Brian was able to win that trophy by bettering all those seventeen and under players at the tournament. He shot a three under par 69.

After the tournament, a pro from the PGA Tour was there to demonstrate how to practice. He gave a clinic and wanted to know who the kid was that shot 69, and out of the crowd came a little guy who was only thirteen years old, besting the likes of the more senior players in the tournament.

The pro wanted Brian to hit a specific target with his shot. Brian got up there and smacked one right at the target, barely missing it. The pro was impressed and said it is always important to hit a target with practice. Brian's score that day at Rolling Hills Country Club was a 69, three under par, and I remember it being one of the best rounds of all the rounds of golf that he had played to date. It was near perfection.

Despite this accomplishment, I did not go around like a chicken with my head cut off, claiming that this guy was the next Tiger Woods. I did not know that he would join the ranks of Tiger Woods and claim a title that he still has today, and it would happen soon after. That's not to say that I thought he was as good as him, but only that he had achieved a level of golf I never expected.

Chapter 9: 1996

Sean O'Hair and John Merrick

"We never know the love of a parent until
we become parents ourselves."

Anonymous

In the San Diego Junior World Tournament, held at the Mission Trails Golf Course for the boys' 13-14 age division, Brian finished in fifth place and was one stroke out of going to Japan again. It was not a big deal. He was over going to Japan and doing well in this significant tournament was more important. His friend from Reno, Nevada, Travis Whisman, won the tournament. He and Brian connected. Travis' mother and father were both teachers, and my wife and I were teachers. We each had a son and a daughter and became friends. That friendship would become very important to us on the way to Stanford, but I will reserve that story for the time it took place instead of getting ahead of myself. Wally Goodwin was also recruiting Travis to go to Stanford. Wally was also interested in another player named Jim Seki from Hawaii. Like Brian, they wanted to play for Stanford.

Finishing in fourth place was John Merrick, who made a 20-foot putt to put himself one stroke ahead of Brian and take the last spot going to Japan. It was not a big deal because the tournament was a total success, and Coach Goodwin congratulated Brian for his success in that tournament.

John Merrick was a player who steadily climbed throughout his golf career. Although he did not win a high school championship, he was a steady player who ended up at the University of California in Los Angeles. John attended Wilson Classical High School, where John won the Moore League High School Championship. Merrick won the Southern California Golf Association Amateur Championship when he was only nineteen years old, making him the youngest person since Tiger Woods in 1994 to capture that title. In 2003, he medaled at the Pac-10 Men's Golf Championships, leading the UCLA Bruins to their first championship victory since 1985. John shot a course-record 63 at Oakmont Glendale, with three eagles in one round, the only collegiate player to do so that year. At the 2002 U. S. Amateur at Oakland Hills, he tied for second in stroke play at three-under par 137 (71-66) and advanced to the second round before losing 2 and 1 to finalist Hunter Mahan.

John had an up-and-down career on tour and has had a conditional status for the past few years. He had a decent streak of keeping his card on the PGA Tour but lost it sometime in 2017. He has had a tough time maintaining his tour card. John has had a decent career for a player who did not set the world on fire with his amateur play. He was not a big winner in his junior or amateur career, but he had a golden touch with the putter, which gave him a lot of success.

Chapter 9: 1996

John was able to win the LA Open, a tournament that he went to as a kid. He was another golfer who became a PGA Tour player from the beginning. John was modestly successful. Although he has won just one tournament on the PGA Tour, he has career earnings of almost ten million dollars. John is still trying out there on tour but needs help making cuts. He was a player who Brian competed against a great deal in local tournaments, and Brian came out ahead much of the time. It was difficult to know who took John to all his tournaments because both parents were quiet like John. I saw his father one time, and he was hiding behind a tree. I never spoke to him, but their support got John to win on the PGA Tour.

Also, for the first time in this tournament, we became aware of a player named Sean O'Hair. Sean could not cut this tournament, shooting a 77-74 in his first two rounds. Sean O'Hair was one of those players who did nothing significant as a junior player and as an amateur, yet he managed to be very successful on the PGA Tour. Imagine that. He did not make a cut at a junior tournament at age fourteen. Yet, he would turn pro by the age of seventeen, dropping out of high school to play on the Nationwide Tour after spending three years training at the Bradenton School of Golf or the David Leadbetter Academy in Bradenton, Florida.

The school is a full-time school for golf, and many parents see it as the "ticket" to the PGA Tour. Many parents spend forty thousand a year for each player to make them good enough to play on the tour, whether the LPGA or the PGA. Sean O'Hair was another player pushed very hard by his dad, which cost them their relationship. However, Sean is still doing well on the PGA Tour. He overcame the early pushing, or did the early pushing make him tough enough to succeed on the PGA?

Sean O'Hair was one of those fantastic surprises in the world of golf. His father, Mark O'Hair, was notorious for being a harsh disciplinarian. After one of the AJGA tournaments Brian and Sean played, we even saw it ourselves. Because Sean had made a bogey or shot over par, his father sent him running, and he was to run until his father told him to stop. Sometimes, he would run as many as eight or nine miles before his dad would pull the plug and let him rest. The discipline issue would eventually become quite contentious and collapse the relationship between them. It became so notorious that his father was interviewed on *60 Minutes* as an example of an overbearing father in sports. I don't think the relationship has recovered despite the success of Sean on the PGA Tour. Sometimes harsh discipline is a blessing for the player, and the death toll on the father. It takes being a parent of an aspiring athlete to understand this.

Aside from winning several local tournaments that summer, Brian capped it off with a victory at the Southern California Junior Golf Association Tournament of Champions at Newport Beach Country Club. Naturally, Brian had an advantage at his club, but the players he competed against had all been winners of tournaments in his 13-14 age group that summer. Winning the tournaments of champions was a big deal, and it was a certainty that he would be the Player of the Year for that age group.

Another highlight that would signal his ability to go low was practice rounds of golf at Newport Beach Country Club, where he managed a 64. Shooting seven under par at that golf course, no matter what the distance, was a significant event. That summer, a guy came to Newport Beach to hit some golf balls, and Brian and I noticed it was Reggie Jackson, the great New York Yankees player. Somehow word got to Reggie that this kid could play magnificent golf, and he sent one of his guys to ask around where this kid was. When the guy asked Brian if he wanted to go out and play a round with him, I told Brian to go ahead and play golf with one of the greatest baseball players of all time. Brian was not as aware of his record as I was, but no matter; he went out and played eighteen holes with him. When he returned, I asked Brian how he did, and he said, "I beat him, Dad." All I could do was laugh. It sounded so funny that this fourteen-year-old could whip this great baseball player on a golf course. Reggie rode up near us and said, "He's a hell of a player, Dad. You should be proud." "I am," I said sheepishly. Reggie drove to his car with his entourage, and we never saw him again.

His best finish at the National Level was second place at the Mission Hills Country Club tournament for 13–14-year-olds put on by the American Junior Golf Association (AJGA). The AJGA is a national tournament where players from all over the country qualify through the application process to show how well they can play. Good play allows them to be eligible for more National tournament play. Brian continued to get better, and his status in Southern California had risen to the top three.

Chapter 10: 1997

Joining the Likes of Tiger Woods

"My dad used to tell me that I have to work twice
as hard as anyone else to prove I'm better."

Tiger Woods

The first year in high school is a tough adjustment for anyone coming from junior high school. As I indicated earlier in this memoir, when Brian was five years old, he took a kind of aptitude test administered by a teacher who had studied an experiment conducted by Harvard and Yale. What the study was able to determine after twenty years of following groups of students from Yale and Harvard is that eighty percent of all athletic and academic scholarships go to the oldest members of their high school graduating class. Because we, as parents, read the study and concluded that it was wise to make our two children the oldest in their ranks, we "held them back" by starting them in kindergarten when they were six or nearly six. The outcome was excellent: Brian got a scholarship to Stanford, and my daughter Jennie got some help (we were too "rich" for her to get more) and went to an excellent college: UC Santa Barbara, which she managed to finish in three and one quarter years.

Starting Brian in kindergarten at age six made a big difference for him by his first year in high school. When the Southern California High School Championships were held, he was fifteen years and nine months, almost sixteen. He was big enough as a first-year student to hit the golf ball a reasonable distance, and he did in his first high school championship at Canyon Country Club in Palm Springs, CA.

It was a hot and challenging day at golf that year as many players were on a course with just eighteen holes, so the play was relatively slow. It took a lot of patience to play well, and after the nearly six-hour round of golf, Brian came out on top with a three under 69 score. He won the Southern Section Individual Boy's Championship. He won by one stroke, but I will let the fine journalistic writing of Martin Beck of the *LA Times* tell the reader the rest of the story. Here is the article he wrote that night for the next day's newspaper.

University Freshman Wins Title

BY MARTIN BECK

MAY 31, 1997 12 AM PT

PALM SPRINGS — "Brian Sinay has won so many junior golf tournaments that he has stopped counting. His father says it's more than 40, including the prestigious Junior World Championship at age 12. So excuse him for not recognizing the significance of the Southern Section individual boys championship until he arrived at Canyon Country Club on Friday.

Sinay, a freshman from University High (in Irvine, CA), got a quick perspective adjustment when he read signs staked in the putting green that listed former champions: Ted Oh, Chris Tidland . . . and, oh yeah, Tiger Woods.

"I felt a little pressure when I saw those names," Sinay said. "Not that I wasn't going to try my hardest to do well anyway. But I thought, 'I want to do well here.' " Sinay did fine, shooting three-under-par 69 to win the title, becoming the first freshman champion since Oh won in 1992. Westlake sophomore J.T. Kohut finished second, one-stroke behind at 70, dropping a shot with a bogey on his final hole.

It was a day of patience and perseverance in the desert, with temperatures pushing 110 degrees, 143 of the section's finest labored through six-hour rounds. There was little wind to provide cooling relief or toughen up the 6,869-yard layout. Two players with some PGA Tour experience appeared ready to take advantage. Culver City junior John Ray Leary, who played in the Buick Invitational in February, made an eagle with a nine-iron shot from 150 yards and got as low as five under before losing five strokes to par on his final four holes. Sunny Hills senior Jin Park played in the 1996 Nissan Open and had three birdies in his first five holes. But he also mixed in a bogey and never got lower than two-under, finishing with a 71. That was good enough for a tie for third place with Servite's Adam Ainbinder, Whitney's David Oh, and Arcadia's Mike Jackson. Those four were called back onto the course for a playoff, and Oh beat out Ainbinder for third with a birdie on the fourth extra hole. Ainbinder, a senior who will play for California next year, also had a chance to challenge for the title. But with four holes to play, he took a double bogey on 18 to go one over. He finished with birdies on his final two holes. Ainbinder said he was lucky to shoot 71. "I was scrambling all day," he said. "I didn't know if the ball was going OB or down the middle, so I was praying on every shot. I only hit two fairways today, one with an iron."

Sinay was much more steady, hitting 10 of 14 fairways and 16 of 18 greens in regulation. The most crucial green he hit was the 17th, and he landed the ball 15 feet from the pin from the rough 130 yards out. The shot cleared a stand of palm trees and a greenside bunker and set up a birdie putt that dropped him to three under with one hole to play.

Scores across the board were lower than usual for a high school tournament on this straightforward course. Two years ago, players shooting 77 played off for the final spots in the CIF-Southern California Golf Assn. Championships. Friday, the playoff was among those who shot 75. Los Alamitos' Brett Dolch and Sunny Hills' Jeff Park were in the playoff, won when Russell Surber of La Canada Flintridge Prep chipped in from the fringe on the second extra hole. Ten Orange County players, including Sinay, Ainbinder, and Jin Park, made it under the wire. Chad Towersey of Corona del Mar and Bret Parker of Mater Dei each shot 72. At 74 were Justin Shapiro of Newport Harbor, Jimmy Pittenger of Santa Margarita, Will Luciano of Servite, Bob Sauer of Mission Viejo, and Steve Bendt of Brea Olinda."

His performance capped a great year of high school golf for Brian. During league golf at University High School, Brian managed to win eleven medalist honors in the team competition. Medalist honors mean that he finished in first place among all players from both teams in individual scoring. For this, he was selected to the first team All-Pacific Coast League. Also, he was established on the First Team, All Orange County, by the *Orange County Register*. He was selected for the same honor by the *LA Times*, First Team, All Orange County. The

LA Times and the *Orange County Register* also awarded him Player of the Year. On a humorous note, his high school coach gave him the Most Improved Player award. I didn't know why a coach would do something like that until I was doing research for this book and I found an article about the coach, Craig Huff, and the comments he made about Ron Won, Brian's teammate. He said that Ron Won was one of the most incredible kids he had ever known. Did the lousy relationship with coaches commence in high school?

This year's additional highlights were his finishes in the CIF Team Regionals at El Niguel Country Club with a field of 72 players; Brian finished fourth. Then at the Team Finals at Saticoy Country Club, Brian finished seventh in an area of 144. Finally, at the CIF-SCGA Team/Individual State Finals (Southern California only at the time), he finished tenth with a score of 72 in a field of 90 players.

Later that summer, Brian qualified for the U.S. Junior Amateur at Auburn Country Club in Auburn, CA. His scores of 75-69/144 won him the first-place medal in the competition. The U.S. Junior Amateur was held at Aronimink Golf Course in Newtown Square, Pennsylvania. He won his first round but lost on the nineteenth hole to a seventeen-year-old headed to Texas University. He did exceptionally well for a fifteen-year-old. Remember, Jack Nicklaus did not win this tournament, but he just got to the semi-finals and lost, which was as close as he came. It didn't matter whether he won that tournament because more players who finished second or worse managed great PGA careers than those who won. Remember that James Oh beat Aaron Baddeley in the finals of the 1998 Junior Amateur?

That summer, he also qualified for the Independent Insurance Agents Junior Classic. Over 13,000 kids around the country try to be eligible for this 160-player field—the top sixty qualify for the last two rounds. Brian finished fifteenth in this tournament with scores of 74-72-75-73 or 294, just six over par. We was seeing a young man with exceptional talent doing quite well for his age. I know he was not setting the world on fire, but he was doing well, and the Stanford coach was there to see this. He was quite impressed with Brian doing as well as he did in a tough tournament with players two years older than him.

He also managed a sixth place finish at the California Junior Amateur among the sixty players who qualified for the finals. Again, this was quite a good showing. His summer also included a round of 66 or 6 under par at Woodley Lakes Golf Course that summer, it was one of his local California Junior Golf Association Tournaments.

He qualified for an American Junior Golf Association tournament in Westminster, Colorado, and finished fifteenth among eighty players with scores of 72-72-73/217, or one over par. This level of playing is the National Junior Amateur circuit, and besides being expensive, it is complicated to even qualify for these tournaments. A player must submit a resume of performances at the local and national levels and hope to be selected for these tournaments. Some of it was political, but most of it was legit. Many of the great players on the PGA Tour were on the AJGA circuit. Brian could only play a few because of the expense, but the guys at Newport Beach Country Club took up two extensive collections for Brian to play significant junior tournaments in his high school career. If any of those great guys manage to read this book, thank you again for supporting Brian. I had Brian write each guy who contributed a personal thank you note.

This was the first year Brian did not qualify for Junior World in San Diego. Past champions should be automatically qualified for the next tournament. When the players reach the

15-17 age range, they must allow in their local region in every state, so players from Idaho are equal in attendance to those from Southern California. Is that stupid or what? There were one hundred players, twenty-five over par for three days. Some were as high as sixty over par! How is that qualifying for the tournament when even par or better will win it? The Junior World people were not sympathetic to the plight of the Southern California players. Brian missed out on qualifying by a single stroke because they limited the number of players from our region! Even though the tournament draws a significant number of good players from around the world, it also allows players who are nearly incompetent to even be in the tournament! We had bitter feelings about that tournament and how it was conducted in the qualifying area. Phil Mickelson never won at the highest level in Junior World. No particular reason, but he did manage to get into all of them in those days.

These were Brian's accomplishments in his freshman year in high school. The two players who played in the pro tournaments in LA and San Diego accomplished less than Brian by the time he was a freshman, so Brian could easily have played at Riviera Country Club and done well. We just never pursued it because his goal was never to get on the PGA tour but to get to Stanford University and play golf for them. Perhaps they needed to work as hard as Tiger.

Freshman Year: 1997

California Interscholastic Federation (CIF) Individual
    Champion 1997 (Southern Section –550 high schools
    represented by 144 players)
Los Angeles Times Orange County 1997 Player of the Year
Orange County Register 1997 Player of the Year

Los Angeles Times First Team: All Orange County 1997
Orange County Register First Team: All Orange County 1997
First Team: All-Pacific Coast League 1997
University High School: Most Improved Player
Medalist Honors: 11

Date	High School Tournament	Finish	Score	Field	Course	Yardage
5/97	CIF Team Regionals	4th	74	72	El Niguel CC	6707
6/97	CIF Team Finals	7th	72	144	Saticoy CC	6883
6/97	CIF Individuals Finals	1st	69	144	Canyon CC	6819
6/97	CIF-SCGA Team/ Individual State Finals	10th	72	90	Rancho California	6722

Date	Local Tournaments	Finish	Score	Field	Course	Yardage
5/97	Anaheim City	1st	68-72	60	Anaheim Hills	6174
6/97	Yorba Linda Invitational	2nd	75-69	60	Yorba Linda CC	6851
7/97	Woodley Lakes Junior	1st	66	120	Woodley Lakes GC	6713
7/97	Big I State Qualifier	7th	72-74	100	DeLaveaga GC	6425

Chapter 11: 1998

Aaron Baddeley and Chasing High School Golf History

"I never had any respect for him ever," he wrote, "except for his lovely, golden, wasted talent."

Hemingway commented in a letter about his friend and fellow writer F. Scott Fitzgerald.

One of the more difficult junior tournaments in Southern California is the L.A. City Championships, which are played during the spring break of the school year, usually in March. This year was challenging, as usual, with 110 players in the 15-17 age group. This tournament can include all of the best players in high school from Southern California who have yet to turn eighteen. Eighteen is when one becomes an amateur, and the junior amateur days are gone. Brian finished second with scores of 73-71-70 in a field of 110 players, and it was a magnificent showing. Brian's childhood nemesis, James Oh, won the tournament. The Wilson and Harding golf courses are where this division played the tournament.

At any point in a young player's golf career, each will encounter players who challenge and make them play better. James Oh was that player for Brian as well as others. Brian was doing that well without the benefit of a recognized golf instructor. At that point, I believe he still needed to start working with Donnie Hill at Strawberry Farms Golf Club in Irvine, just down the hill from where we lived. Although the high school team played their home matches at that club, Donnie did not become his teacher until Brian's junior year in high school. Brian was doing well, and he was doing it with his swing. His short game was outstanding, and his putting was just incredible. Donnie Hill, the former Angel's baseball player turned golf instructor, was hired by the owner of Strawberry Farms Golf Club, Doug DeCinces, another great former Angel baseball player. Getting good golf instruction is a matter of how much one wants to pay, and although Donnie Hill was not a top-caliber instructor by any means, he was convenient and an excellent golfer.

In retrospect, I didn't know how much time and effort great golf teachers had made before becoming as good as they were: David Leadbetter, Jim McClean, Hank Haney, and Butch Harmon all had extensive experience in the analysis of the golf swing for that time. Donnie Hill was "studying" the golf swing at the time, and I believe he was trying to teach a Ben Hogan-like swing to Brian, who did not have Ben Hogan's physical skills. Ben Hogan was very flexible, with long arms, a thin body, tight hips, tremendous "lag" (very supple wrists) in the downward portion of the golf swing, and so on. Brian was not doing any of that. I learned that I lacked knowledge about the swing. It is challenging to be an expert in something that complicated. It did not hurt him, but it was not the swing for him.

Even though Brian would win his second high school championship with the tutoring of Donnie Hill, there were some fundamental problems with the swing. When Brian struggled at Stanford, all I could hear from Donnie Hill was that Brian was "too stiff" as a player. In other words, his body was too stiff and did not create the whip that great players like Hogan did. That is Donnie Hill not accepting responsibility for his failings as an instructor. Players with a body build like Brian were successful because they had better instruction than Brian. Donnie Hill thinks he knew the golf swing, but he was just learning what it was at the time he taught Brian. Did Donnie Hill know about "shallowing" the golf club and pronation through the hitting area? What knowledge he did have was far exceeded by the knowledge he didn't have.

That year, the Southern Section CIF high school championship was again held at Canyon Country Club in Palm Springs. They stuck Brian's name as a tournament champion in the ground along with all the other past winners. It was quite a sight to see. It was better weather that year, the round went quickly, and players came to play. James Oh finished first with a score of 67, and John Leary was second place with a 70. Brian finished fifth with a score of 73, and there were 144 players from all the best schools in the Southern California region. This region has 583 high schools compared to most states. This region was just the Southern Region or Southern California. California did not have a state championship at the time, but I believe they do now.

The odd thing about the tournament is that there is no big award ceremony. The players gather on the patio and watch the scores as one group walks back to the clubhouse. It is quite a championship, though, and almost anyone would want to win, if not only for the history books.

Brian again qualified for the Junior World tournament in San Diego and played as a sixteen-year-old in the 15-17 age group. Players who are seventeen through the middle of July are also able to compete. Depending on their birth date, some players can be a year or two older. There were 232 players in this age group from all over the world. Taro Hiroi won the tournament with a four under par 284. The tournament was played on the South and North courses at Torrey Pines Golf Course in La Jolla, CA. Brian finished in fifty-fifth place but did not qualify for the last round. He missed the cut by one stroke. A golfer named Aaron Baddeley finished third.

Perhaps the most gratifying experience that summer was qualifying for the U.S. Junior Amateur tournament at the Stanford Golf Course. With Wally Goodwin nearby, he managed to get us a caddy for the tournament. After the first round, Brian shot 77 and was close to qualifying but needed a much better score to qualify for the Conway Farms Golf Course trip in Lake Forest, Illinois. He went to the range for a warm-up before the second round, and I noticed one thing he could do to help improve his ball striking. Whatever I said, and I honestly can't remember, Brian managed an eagle on the difficult 12th hole and an even par 71 in the second round to qualify for the Junior Amateur. It was a happy flight home. He had qualified for the Junior Amateur for the second time. There were 156 players from around the country from a field of over four thousand players. That was an accomplishment. It is rarefied air. The Junior Amateur is the tournament that determines who the best junior player in the country was at that time.

Chapter 11: 1998

We ran into a brutal wind in the first round when we got to the tournament, and Brian shot a 77. He shot a 71 in the second round and qualified for match play. The top sixty-four players allow for match play, with the number one seed playing the number sixty-four seed and on down the line.

Brian managed to win two rounds, first the top sixty-four and then the top thirty-two, to get to the quarterfinals or the top sixteen. When one gets to the round of sixteen, coaches from around the country come to look at those players. The best college golf schools come to see if they can check out the players and send them letters of interest. I watched them as they passed the line and looked at the player's swings. Brian's friend, Travis Whisman, was hitting golf balls not too far from Brian when an assistant coach pulled the head coach of Oklahoma State to watch Travis hit balls. "Look at that lag!" the associate coach exclaimed to the head coach. Little did they know that they had no chance of getting Travis. He was headed to the University of Nevada at Las Vegas. We didn't know that at the time, but it will be an integral part of the story about Brian and Stanford.

In the quarterfinals, Brian was almost sixteen, but his opponent was nearly eighteen, and he lost to him 2 and 1. If Brian had won, Brain could have faced James Oh in the semi-finals. It would have been great to see them play against each other again. I know that James would not want to have faced Brian. Brian had no fear of James Oh. James Oh once told me, "I think Brian is so good." I don't think he ever told Brian that. I don't think Brian ever knew how good he was. It would eventually turn out to be an F.S. Fitzgerald kind of thing.

James Oh won the tournament, beating Aaron Baddeley 1 up. Aaron was the medalist with a score of 135, nine under par! And remember, he did it with incredible winds blowing the first day. Perhaps it was why Brian got down on his knees and bowed to Aaron at the end of the second round. He learned that one could be good at this game while others are better. I still have a picture in my head of him doing that. It was honorable, but it also spoke to a kind of resignation that he could not do as well at one time or another. But he would. The following year in high school was his greatest ever.

Even though James Oh beat Aaron Baddeley, Baddeley ended up becoming a much better pro in the long run. He won the Australian Open at nineteen, the youngest ever to do so, but he was an amateur. Aaron won it again the following year, and his career as a professional golfer took off. He won ten tournaments worldwide and over twenty million dollars.

We saw Aaron at the San Diego Open one year, but he did not see us. He was playing, and it just isn't right to say, "Hey, do you remember Brian Sinay bowing down to you in that U.S. Amateur in 1998?" Something like that would go over like a lead balloon. Despite his excellent career, he was overshadowed by Adam Scott, a more accomplished Australian player. Aaron's dad had told me that Aaron wanted to be a professional golfer from when he was a young kid. He had excellent skills, and one of them was his incredible putting. It is surprising that he didn't accomplish more. The support his parents gave to him was great since they traveled from Australia for Aaron to compete in junior and amateur tournaments. How's that for dedication?

Here are the results of Brian's tournament play in 1998, his sophomore year in high school.

Local Tournaments:

Date	Tournament	Scores	Place	Field	Location	Yardage
3/98	L.A. City Championship	73-71-70	2nd	110	Griffith Park GC	6947
6/98	Yorba Linda Invitational	70-74	1st	60	Yorba Linda CC	6851
7/98	Mesa Verde Junior	71	1st	50	Mesa Verde CC	6733
7/98	Maxfli Local Qualifier	68	2nd	60	Ironwood CC	6850
7/98	Maxfli Regional Qualifier	71-74	2nd	40	Lakeside CC	6850

National Tournaments:

Date	Tournament	Scores	Place	Field	Location	Yardage
5/98	US Open Local Qualifier	70	1st	84	Victoria CC	6483
6/98	US Open Sectionals	78-77	45th	120	Lake Merced CC	6807
6/98	AJGA Mission Hills	68-75-78	18th	100	Mission Hills CC	6906
7/98	US Junior Qualifier	77-71	3rd	104	Stanford GC	6786
7/98	US Junior Amateur	79-71	Top 16	156	Conway Farms CC	6721
7/98	Junior World	74-77-75	55th	232	Torrey Pines GC	6900

Date	Tournament	Scores	Place	Field	Location	Yardage
8/98	Scott Robertson	74-71-69	8th	100	Roanoke CC	6500
12/98	Doral Publix Junior Classic	74-74-78	21st	225	Doral Golf Resort	6701

High School Competition:

Date	Tournament	Scores	Place	Field	Location	Yardage
5/98	CIF Team Regionals	73	2nd	72	El Niguel CC	6707
6/98	CIF Team Finals	73	5th	144	Canyon CC	6819
6/98	CIF Team Regionals	74	10th	72	El Prado GC	6671
6/98	CIF Individuals Finals	73	5th	72	Friendly Hills CC	6412
6/98	CIF-SCGA Team/ Individual State Finals	72	4th	90	Rancho California	6722

Chapter 12: 1999

Sergio Garcia, Ty Tryon, and Taking Down a Tiger Woods' Record

"I always outworked everybody. Work never bothered me like it bothers some people."

Ben Hogan

Despite winning the CIF Championship as a freshman, Brian still had to qualify for the tournament in a regional contest for all-league players in their respective high school leagues. It was a challenging course in Southern California, and the competition was quite challenging. Brian had qualified for his third Southern California high school championship, but he did not set the world on fire with his score of 76. While we were walking to the parking lot, a parent who knew Brian and I said aloud, "It was pretty tough out there, Brian. Are you ready for the championship?" Brian immediately responded, "I'll be ready for it, don't worry."

The day came in May of 1999 when Brian went to Canyon Country Club in Palm Springs to play for his second CIF High School Championship. He had worked hard on his game hitting hundreds of balls every day. I will let Peter Yoon of the *LA Times* tell the story because he does it better than I can.

Sinay Attacks the Course Like Tiger in Record 65

BY PETER YOON

MAY 21, 1999, 12 AM

When guys with walkie-talkies drive up in golf carts to follow a player in a high school golf tournament, it's pretty clear that something special is taking place. As word began to spread through Canyon Country Club in Palm Springs about Brian Sinay's sizzling round in the Southern Section Boys' Individual championship Thursday, that's precisely what happened. With each stroke, they reported back to their home base. Residents watching from backyards along the fairways took note and whispered over the fences like a game of telephone. "He's five under." "He's six under." The gallery swelled. So did the number after the minus sign. And when it was over, Sinay had made history.

The University High junior shot a seven-under-par 65 to win his second section title in three years and break the tournament record of 66 set by Tiger Woods in 1994. Sinay, who also won at Canyon as a freshman in 1997, said everything was right for him Thursday. His swing felt good, the greens were in mint condition, the sky was bright blue and there was no hint of a breeze. "I just felt like I couldn't miss a shot," Sinay said. "I thought I could birdie every hole." Sinay started on the seventh hole in the shotgun format. He birdied four of his first six holes and the record chase was on. Woods, who won three Southern Section titles, set the record at La Cumbre Country Club in Santa Barbara with a 67. Woods won his other two titles at Canyon, shooting 68 each time. "I tried not to think about numbers, but it was hard," said Sinay, who bettered his previous low round by a stroke. "I just calmed myself down and slowed down and then I wasn't nervous anymore for the last three holes." Sinay, who had eight birdies and a bogey, could have gone even lower. He barely missed a six-foot birdie putt on his 13th hole and missed a 2 1/2-footer for birdie on his 16th. After a birdie on his 17th put him eight under, he rolled a 12-foot birdie putt three feet past the hole on his last hole and missed the putt coming back for his only bogey. "It was a tough finish," he said. "Sometimes those small ones are harder than the long ones."

Scoring conditions were ideal, and the results showed it. Sinay's teammate, Ron Won, finished second with a bogey-free round of 66. Defending section champion James Oh of Lakewood was third at 67. In all, six players were under 70, and the cut to make the CIF-SCGA finals fell at two over. Won figured 66 might win the title but wasn't disappointed. "If anybody beats me, I want it to be him," Won said. "He's, my teammate." Ryan Miller, the third University player on the field, shot 74, giving the Trojans a three-player team score of 11-under-par. The Trojans were still seething about shooting a season-worst five-player score of 46-over-par 406 in brutal winds during the Southern Section team finals last week at La Purisima. The Trojans, and the six other regional champions, had late-morning tee times at the course with notorious afternoon winds and were unhappy about it. None of the seven top-seeded teams advanced to the CIF-SCGA finals. "I guess you could say we made a statement about how messed up things were at La Purisima," Won said.

Woods (1991, '93, and '94), Boots Porterfield of Long Beach Wilson (1942-44), and Mac Hunter of Santa Monica (1945-47) are the only players to win three section titles. Brian Sinay of the University is the second golfer from Orange County to win more than one Southern Section individual championship. (Along with Tiger Woods). A list of the champions from the county, with school, course, and score (the title was decided by match play until 1943).

1936 Jack Robinson, Santa Ana (Montebello GC) 1 up
1940 Douglas May, Santa Ana (Montebello GC) 3 and 2
1959 Fred Murray, Capistrano Valley (Hesperia CC) 74
1968 Scott Pomeroy, San Clemente (Hacienda GC) 72
1971 Roger Calvin, Los Amigos (California CC) 74
1988 Matt Baugh, Huntington Beach (Mission Hills CC) 72
1989 Chris Tidland, Valencia (Canyon CC) 72
1991 Tiger Woods, Western (Canyon CC) 68
1993 Tiger Woods, Western (Canyon CC) 68
1994 Tiger Woods, Western (La Cumbre CC) 66
1997 Brian Sinay, University (Canyon CC) 69
1999 Brian Sinay, University (Canyon CC) 65.

What can you say about a kid who beats a Tiger Woods record? While I watched Brian play the last hole, the club pro came over to me and said, "Dad, these were the same pin placements for Tiger the two times he won this championship here. He shot 68 both times. A 65 is outstanding, and you should be proud." I thanked him for that information and told him I would share it with Brian. We all headed back to the club-house, a big group of people following and mumbling about what they had just seen. He would have had a 64 if not for the three-putt on the last hole. But it was the record, nonetheless. It was incredible, nonetheless.

I caught up with Brian and told him he had beaten Tiger Woods' record. He was not overly thrilled about it, but he humbly accepted it. I asked him if he liked this kind of competition and winning a major golf tournament like this. He said over his shoulder because I was a pace or two behind him, "It's okay, Dad." Just, okay? Just, okay? It was one of the moments in the history of golf with Brian that I realized he did not love golf. I loved golf more than he did. I read books and the history of it and all of that. He did not have such a book in his room. Steve Conway did just like the other players looking to become PGA Tour pros; they surrounded themselves with golf literature. Brian had none. It was not something I ever expected him to do, but I thought he might take the hint that perhaps he could try with his ability.

I asked Brian that question to see if he had any idea of pursuing it for a livelihood, but he would only make that clear once Peter Yoon interviewed him just before his last high school tournament in May of 2000. Did I want him to be a pro? No, after this performance, he could be one, and he could be a successful one, certainly nowhere near the ability of Tiger Woods, but a decent, respectable pro on tour. He was performing at the level of those contemporary players who had done well on time. Despite this accomplishment, it did not move his thinking about a future with golf. It was always about getting to Stanford, his only obsession. Sometimes a dad just does not see what is happening right before him. I know this now because I wrote this in retrospect.

Brian qualified for that summer's American Junior Golf Association Tournament of Champions. They held it on the Scarlett Course at Ohio State University. While Brian was playing his second round of golf, a coach approached me and asked me if the young man on the course in front of us was someone I knew. "Well, coach, that's my son, Brian Sinay." He then asked me if he would like me to come to Ohio State and play golf for him. His name was Jim Brown, and we immediately hit it off because his name was Jim Brown. The coach said that Brian must have some connection to Ohio if he was wearing a Cleveland Indians hat. Brian was a sports fan, and since I had taught him to like the Cleveland Indians because I was a fan as a child, I told the coach about my background and history. I told him I was born in Canton, Ohio, and grew up in Buckeye until my dad moved us to California when I was twelve. I told him I had maintained my allegiance to Ohio because I grew up with Jim Brown, the Cleveland Browns, Rocky Colavito, and the Cleveland Indians. Now the coach was excited because he thought it would be easy for Brian to want to be a player at Ohio State since that had been the college of choice for Jack Nicklaus, Tom Weiskopf, Joey Sindelar, Ted Tryba, and Ed Sneed.

I told the coach that I would introduce Brian to him and that if he could convince him to go to Ohio State, I would be all for it. The coach took Brian aside, talked to him for a few minutes, and then wandered back to me and said, "How long has he had this obsession with going to Stanford?" I told him it started in the sixth grade, and like a bulldog, he had not lost his focus on going there, come hell or high water. The coach thanked me for his time, gave me his card, and said that if Brian had a change of heart, he had a place for him at Ohio State. After the success of winning a second Southern

Chapter 12: 1999

California High School Championship, it was common for coaches to extend an invitation for Brian to play golf for their colleges: He had verbal offers from UCLA, USC, Ohio State, North Carolina, Pepperdine, and many others. Brian turned a blind eye to all of them.

Along with this tournament, Brain qualified for the Western Junior tournament in Gaylord, Michigan, at the Tree Tops Resort. It was a short course, and scores were low, with Brian shooting a 65 in the first round to take the lead in the tournament.

In the tournament was a player by the name of Ty Tryon. He was born in Raleigh, North Carolina, and coached by David Leadbetter at the Academy in Florida at a very young age. He was three years younger than Brian at the time of this tournament. I believe he won the tournament, and his mother went catatonic. She called her husband and acted like Ty had won the Masters. Just three years later, Ty would turn pro at age sixteen, which caused a great deal of controversy since many players go through their college days to "earn" their respect as players at the amateur levels. But Ty was exceptional, at least momentarily, and cut at sixteen at the PGA Tour's Honda Classic. He was still an amateur but turned pro after this tournament. He was "ready" for the PGA Tour and qualified twenty-third in the fall of 2001 for the tour.

He signed a lucrative endorsement deal with Callaway, estimated at several million dollars. In his first entire season on the tour, he did not make but one cut and battled mononucleosis. By the end of the 2003 season, he had made 125,000 dollars and finished 196th on the PGA's money list. For several years, he struggled to make a living on any tour. I tell this story only to point out that parents can be overzealous about their kid's golfing abilities. He might have been more successful if he had developed more as a player in the junior ranks and amateur. He has the moniker of being one of the greatest "flameouts" in golf history.

It was the same with Michele Wei. Her parents pushed her to be on the LPGA too early, and although she had successes, it might have been better had she had more time to mature as a player. Despite receiving a large amount of money when she joined the LPGA, her accomplishments paled compared to her talent. It was the same kind of overzealous behavior on the part of Mike Oh, the father of James Oh, who thought that turning pro would lead to success when it did not. I guess it is just a gamble; some win, and some lose. They all just reach a different rung of the ladder. They all hold onto the "Golden Ring" for different periods of time.

The tournament went fine for Brian and his friend Travis Whisman, and we took the long drive back to the Detroit airport with questions from Travis about how to play a particular shot. Players at that age did not realize the complexity of manipulating the golf ball to get it to do what you wanted. It takes high-level instruction for players to play shots they usually would not know how to play. I realized that none of these players who intended to play on the tour had the skills that others were getting, including the likes of Ty Tryon, and despite getting that level of instruction, there still needed to be guaranteed for performance. Other factors include having ice run through one's veins instead of blood, putting a putt under extreme pressure, or having the maturity to handle the pressures of golf competition. One must be pretty unaffected by the emotional element of golf. Playing in these tournaments was accepted as "normal" by these players, but the overall expense was quite significant even for those days. If a kid grows up as a prince, what does he know about a kid who grew up in poverty?

Chapter 12: 1999

Perhaps the highlight of Brian's experience that summer was a trip to The Junior Orange Bowl International Golf Championship at the Biltmore Golf Course in Coral Gables, Florida. The competition is similar to the Junior World International Competition in San Diego each year, and it is the east coast version of the same tournament. It is a "major" junior tournament because players come from around the world to compete. We learned when we got there that Sergio Garcia, the young Spaniard who had won many junior tournaments and was destined to be a star, was to compete in it. "There goes the first place," I said to Brian. Anyway, the good people of Newport Beach Country Club did a great deal to get us there, and Brian wrote individual thank-you notes before we left for Coral Gables, Florida.

The significant part was that Brian was randomly selected to play with Sergio and a young man from Thailand for the first two rounds. It was just an unreal stroke of luck to be paired with him. It was so exciting to see this because Sergio was playing in his last junior tournament, one that he had not won, and he came one last time just to try and win this tournament. The first round commenced, and I was more nervous than Brian watching him play toe to toe with Sergio. Each tee shot of Brian's with the driver fell about 20 yards short of Sergio, yet Brian was a bigger guy than Sergio and about three inches taller. Knowledge like this is why good professional instruction is necessary for any junior golfer aspiring to make it on the PGA tour. Sergio was taught by his European Tour player father, and the chances of Brian competing successfully against a player who has had that kind of instruction were not good. But by the end of the first round, it was only a one-stroke difference. Sergio shot even par, and Brian shot one over par.

How did Brian manage that score with twenty yards different from Sergio's drives? It was Brian's short game. Brian's putting was excellent, and he got up and down when needed. During that first round, I walked along, and a gentleman to my left asked, "Is that your son playing with Sergio?" I said, "Yes, the big boy who makes Sergio look small, but he is still out driving Brian by 20 to 30 yards." "Yes, that would be because of Sergio's lag," said the gentleman. That is where I discovered my lack of golf knowledge. I turned and introduced myself, "Dick Sinay." The gentleman introduced himself as John Inman, the University of North Carolina head coach. "Lag" made the difference in the distance separation between Brian and Sergio. Sadly, it reminded me of the question I asked Brian's first teacher, "What exactly should the wrists be doing during the golf swing?" "What wrists?" quipped Brian's first instructor. I was learning that Brian was doing well despite not being taught much about it. Not knowing how the wrists behave in the golf swing is like not knowing who the President is. Knowing therefore that outstanding instruction is essential from the right teachers.

Sergio Garcia was one of the first players in a long time to have his swing compared to Ben Hogan's swing. Now that is quite a compliment. Why so? Well, Hogan had a beautiful "lag" in his downswing, which essentially is a delay of the release of the golf club, which ensures a more significant impact on the golf ball. It is a bit more complicated than that, but one can say that Sergio was exercising it and Brian Sinay was not. Thus, the distance problem. Even so, the University of North Carolina coach asked if he could talk to Brian after the round and see if he might like to play for the Tar Heels. I told the coach that Brian had had his mind set on going to Stanford since he was in the sixth grade, and even though he was welcome to approach him, it was just to find out how committed he was to be going there. The coach did not bother Brian, and I thanked him for letting me know why the difference in the two distances existed between the golfers and wandered away to meet Brian. I talked to Brian after the round, and he said he had a great time playing with Sergio.

The second round went fine for Brian but better for Sergio. I think he shot a five under 67, and Brian could only manage another 72, but it did allow him to play the last two days of the four-day tournament. Sergio was off to win the tournament in the next few days, and Brian was just trying to make a respectable showing. During the tournament's second round, Brian could be seen walking down the fairway with this future superstar and chatting away with Sergio. It was an incredible experience for him and one he will never forget. He told me Sergio was charming and friendly to him, and they talked about many things while playing. Imagine that.

That summer, Brian received a phone call from Wally Goodwin, who offered a sixty percent scholarship to Brian. Brian was ecstatic. I wasn't. I thought he deserved more, but because this was his dream, we said nothing. We were elated that Brian had reached his goal of being offered a golf scholarship at Stanford. However, it was not long after that another phone call came from Wally. I cannot recall the time before the second phone call, but the time-lapse was insignificant. It was about a month or two after he received the scholarship that the second call came rescinding it. When Wally called to rescind the scholarship, I was not at home. I came home from teaching a class at night to find Brian sullen and depressed. My wife told me that Wally Goodwin had taken away the scholarship offer. My only reaction was to say, "Why?" Everything was speculative at this point, and I was beyond bothered by this news. Brian had called his friend Travis who also had been recruited by Wally and told him the events that had transpired. Travis was somehow able to reach Wally and talk to him. Travis was distraught that Wally had taken away Brian's scholarship. I am not sure why Wally rescinded Brian's scholarship, but Travis was so upset by Brian's loss that he called Wally and talked to him about why it was so important to give Brian the scholarship he had worked for all these years. I believe the phone call to Wally from Travis made a great deal of difference because I would learn from Wally the next day that he had spoken to Travis and the appeal he made to Wally got him to change his mind.

Wally recruited three Stanford team players that year: Brian Sinay, Jim Seki, and Travis Whisman. Wally felt that the three would be the nucleus of another National Championship team for Stanford. Brian and Jim Seki accepted the scholarships, but Travis did not. He rejected the offer by Wally Goodwin, and Wally was quite surprised by that. Wally was led to believe but never told that Travis always had intentions of going to the University of Nevada in Las Vegas. Travis liked the coach there and thought that since the school had recently produced some good PGA Tour pros, he would like to be in line to be the next one.

Travis had always had the intent to play on the PGA Tour. Travis felt his best chance to play on the tour was at UNLV. Wally was upset at Travis for not taking the scholarship. We thought Wally took it away from Brian because he did not get what he wanted. We were never sure why Wally rescinded Brian's scholarship, as no reason was given when he did it.

I was in my classroom when the phone call came from Wally Goodwin, and I stepped outside the room to talk to Wally. I asked him why he rescinded Brian's scholarship since he had worked hard for six years to prove he could play golf for

Stanford, and Wally was sheepish and embarrassed by what he had done. Wally told me that his conversation with Travis had altered his thinking, and he would like to reinstate the offer if Brian was willing to accept it. Then he asked me if Brian would be as hard a worker at Stanford as he had been to get there. I assured the coach that that would be the case. I had promised him that Brian would be as diligent as he had been in getting to Stanford, and I had no notions that it would be otherwise.

Wally then indicated that he would be in touch about a trip to Stanford to be shown around in the future. I got off the phone with him and felt tremendous relief knowing that Brian could go to Stanford on the golf scholarship for which he had worked so hard. In 1999, there were no cell phones, but I could call my wife (an elementary school teacher) and tell her secretary to pass on the word to her. In any case, dinner that night at the Sinay's house was much more pleasant. All's well that ends well. But it was not the end, only the beginning. I had kept in mind that Wally wanted to be sure that Brian would work hard on his golf at Stanford. I never told Brian that I had told the coach that he was expecting the same effort at Stanford that he made to get there. It was all part of our poor communication.

Some weeks later, the family made a trip to Stanford and met Wally, who graciously took us around the campus and showed us a great time. It was quite a bit more optimistic than the recent phone calls. During our time with Wally, he indicated to Brian that he would play him in all eleven tournaments in his freshman year. Wally had that kind of confidence in Brian's game. He also indicated that he would increase his scholarship to seventy percent, a ten percent increase from the original offer. Again, as parents, we said nothing and did not challenge the request (we thought he deserved ninety percent) because we knew how important this was to Brian. We did not want to shake the boat or call out the coach for offering so little for a player of Brian's caliber. We were willing to pay the difference to see Brian live his dream. After all, he nearly tied the three high school championships of Tiger Woods and did better Tiger's high school score of 66 by one stroke.

Wally thought that Brian would be a great player for Stanford. When Brian got there in the fall of the following year, he stood on the first tee, hit his drive, and Wally Goodwin turned to the new coach of Stanford, Jeff Mitchell, and said, "Coach, there is your next NCAA Division I Champion from Stanford." Why would he say it if he didn't believe it? After all, he had coached Tiger Woods for two years.

Here are the results of his golf tournament in 1999:

Junior Year: 1999

California Interscholastic Federation (CIF) Individual
    Champion (Southern Section –550 high schools) **Score
    of 65 broke the CIF record of Tiger Woods*
*Orange County Register: 1999 Co-Player of the Year
Orange County Register: First Team-All Orange County 1999
Los Angeles Times First Team: All Orange County 1999
Irvine Worlds News: Athlete of the Week First Team:
    All-Pacific Coast League 1999 University High School:
    Co-Most Valuable Player 1999
Medalist Honors: 11
SCPGA All-Southern California Junior Team 1999

High School Competition:

Date	Tournament	Place	Scores	Field	Location	Yardage
5/99	Pacific Coast League finals	2nd	141	36	El Dorado GC	6698
5/99	CIF Team Regionals	1st	69	120	Mesquite CC	6500
5/99	CIF Team Finals	7th	75	120	La Purisima GC	6657
5/99	CIF Individuals Finals	1st	65	72	Canyon CC	6819

National Level Competition:

Date	Tournament	Place	Scores	Field	Location	Yardage
4/99	AJGA Scottsdale	17th	75-78	153	Grayhawk GC	6950
6/99	AJGA Mission Hills	24th	79-78-69	226	Mission Hills CC	7025
6/99	AJGA Oklahoma	25th	76-79-70	225	Oak Tree CC	6784
7/99	US Junior Am Qualifier	7th	71-76	147	Stanford GC	6850
7/99	AJGA Rolex TOC	26th	75-72 -75-72	294	Ohio State GC	7105
7/99	Western Junior	26th	65-73 -69-73	280	Treetops Resort	6280
7/99	AJGA Coto De Caza	8th	72-74-75	221	Coto De Caza CC	6975
8/99	US Am Qualifier	7th	72-75	147	Tustin Ranch GC	6855

Chapter 13: 2000

Dyeing Out to Make Southern California High School History

"Sons always have a rebellious wish to be
disillusioned by that which charmed their fathers."

Aldous Huxley

It was May 21, 2000, Brian's senior year in high school. He had a chance to make Southern California High School Golf history by winning his third high school individual championship at Canyon Country Club in Palm Springs. Canyon Country Club was the site of his two previous victories, including a record-breaking 65 last year. Peter Yoon of the *LA Times* sports reporting for high school golf asked Brian for an interview. Peter's article was so good and revealing about Brian that I have to share it. It's essential to our understanding of what happened to Brian when he went to Stanford in the fall of the same year. Sometimes a father is too close to see what's happening in front of him.

"Dyeing to Win"

BY PETER YOON

MAY 21, 2000

"The big day is approaching, and Brian Sinay's biggest concern is his hair. Well, that and which pants he is going to wear. The brown roots of his bleached blond hair have crept into view, and Sinay wonders whether he should dump another batch of dye on his head before he tees it up on Monday at Canyon Country Club in Palm Springs, looking to make history one more time at the Southern Section individual championships."

"The 18-year-old senior from University High (Irvine) leans back in his chair, dropping the Styrofoam cup he's been shredding piece by piece before grasping the spiky surfer hairdo in contemplation. 'I don't know,' he says, 'What do you think?'

"He did this last year, too, dyeing his hair blond just before the postseason. He said he wanted to be different. As if his golf game wouldn't stand out on its own"

"Last year, Sinay shot seven-under-par 65 to win the title and break the Southern record of 66 set by Tiger Woods. Monday, he will try to match another record. Sinay, who also won as a freshman in 1997, is poised to become only the fourth player to win three section titles since the tournament began in 1931. Only Woods, who won in '91, '93, and '94 while at Western High, has done it in the last half-century. Boots Porterfield of Long Beach Wilson (1942-1944) and Mac Hunter of Santa Monica (1945-1947) were the others. Right now, setting records is of no concern to Sinay, the No. 33 ranked junior player in the nation. Forgetting his hair for the moment, Sinay turns his attention to another pressing problem. Last Monday, a sign posted at the section's regional qualifying tournament read 'No Cargo Pants Allowed at Canyon.' Cargo pants, those baggy cotton trousers with oversized pockets in the legs, are a staple of Sinay's wardrobe. He wears them to school, he wears them to parties, and he wears them while playing golf. Last year, he wore them at Canyon, contributing to his reputation as a golf rebel."

'He looks like a typical skater-type guy,' said Ron Won, a Stanford freshman who played with Sinay at University for three years. 'You look at him, and you're like, 'You golf? Yeah, right.' 'He wears those weird army-type pants, but it's unique. He is proud to be who he is and is not ashamed.'

Peter continued, "The mischievous part of Sinay wants to show up Monday wearing cargo pants. What are they going to do, keep the defending champ from playing? But the rational side knows it's best not to make waves."

'I don't think I own a pair of regular Khakis,' Sinay said. 'I guess I'm going to have to buy a new pair of pants.'

"Unlike many top junior players, Sinay is not an obsessed range rat. When he feels like he spends too much time playing and practicing, he goes to the beach, listens to music, or hangs out with friends instead."

'If I had gone the golf route the entire year, I don't know if I'd still be playing,' Sinay said. 'I'm the type of guy that would get frustrated with too much of it. I'd rather not necessarily be that tied to it. I don't want to make it my life.'

"So other than Saturday morning rounds at Newport Beach Country Club, Sinay has been devoting many of his recent weekends to activities not related to golf. Weightlifting and pickup basketball are normal parts of his routine, and social activities such as movies and rock concerts are necessary. In December, he saw Rage Against the Machine, and he ranks Barely Legal, a punk band composed of some of his friends from University High, as his favorite group. At a recent Blink-182 concert, he ventured into the mosh pit."

'I am not one of those guys that want to bash people around,' he said. 'I don't even know what you do in the mosh pit, and it was just something to try.'

"That is not to say golf has taken a backseat to anything, and its still Sinay's top priority. He began playing at age 8, started serious competition soon after, and won the Junior World Championship at age 12. His practice sessions are as thorough as any of the top players when he's focused. Before big tournaments, like Mondays, he will spend hours a day at the driving range and putting green, ensuring everything is just right. But off time is."

'He's a lot more casual about golf than most guys,' Won said. 'So many of these guys are rotating their life around golf, but…. Brian is enjoying life.'

"Sinay's flair for variety can be traced to his parents. Dick and Heidi Sinay try to keep the golf pressure out of the house. Golf talk at the dinner table is limited, and practice is encouraged but never required."

'We try to be low-key about golf,' Dick Sinay said. 'My theory is that you expose kids to different things and let them choose what they want to do. Brian loved golf.'

"As a young boy, Sinay had heard about a college in Northern California that his friend called "cool." That's how he became interested in, then obsessed with, Stanford. He got a Stanford sweatshirt in the fourth [6th—my brackets] grade and, about the same time, set his sights on earning a golf scholarship from the university. He never considered other schools."

'It took precedence over everything else,' Brian said.

"The good news came about seven months ago. Stanford offered him a golf scholarship. The scholarship, it turned out, was the easy part. Sinay still had to be accepted to the university. But his impeccable academic records passed muster with the Stanford admissions committee, which accepted Sinay a few weeks later. He wasn't prepared for the hint of depression that came with fulfilling his longtime dream."

'My only real goal was to get a scholarship to Stanford,' Sinay said. When it works out, it's nice, but it's also kind of a letdown. You've done everything you wanted to do and then reached your goal; from there, it's hard to keep going. It's like, what do I do now?"

Peter continued, "One thing left to do is play in the Southern Section tournament. Sinay's eyes light up when the topic shifts to Canyon Country Club. He talks about where he will sleep. His uncle owns a cabin in Palm Springs and has stayed there, in the primary bedroom, the night before each of his section titles. He will do so again tonight. He talks about that magical, record-setting day last spring and can't hide the pride in his humble smile when he's mentioned in the same sentence as Tiger Woods. He remembers the control he felt on the course that day, the weather conditions, and every shot he took. But most of all, he remembers the greens."

"Those greens are perfect,' he said. 'If you miss a putt there, it's your fault, end of the story. That's all there is to it. It might not be your stroke, it could be your read, but it's not the greens.' said Brian.

"Can his 65, or even his championship, be duplicated?" Sinay isn't counting on it. There are too many good players to contend with. And in a one-day tournament, it will depend on who has their game in the best shape for 4 1/2 hours at 8 A.M. Monday.``

'I'm not going to think about winning,' he said. 'For any player, even the best players, the odds of winning are slim. As it is, I have already beaten the odds, and I've beaten the odds twice. If I beat them again, I don't know what to do.''

"His thoughts wander to the course and the lake sitting in front of the 18th green."

'I'll jump in that lake,' he proclaimed. 'I'll jump in that lake.'

"Brand new Khaki pants, bleached-blond hair and all."

There are several takeaways from the article that I want to reflect upon. When one is a parent who is working full time, it is difficult even to have time to talk to your kid when one has so much to do. I read the article, and it validated my knowledge about Brian's attitude toward golf. He was not in love with it, and I enjoyed it more than he did. At one time or another, his sister told me that Brian thought golf was a "stupid game." His comment came sometime after Stanford. He had shown a motivation to play the game, but he never saw himself playing it even when he got to Stanford, much less after that.

My second takeaway is that it was apparent to me that he was choosing values that I was not even aware of: listening to hard rock, following bands that were weird and out of the norm like Rage Against the Machine, which is just a rebellious hard rock group that tells kids don't do what your parents want you to do and go against the norm. Brian had already "gone against the norm" when he showed up to play in the high school championship the year before: he had dyed his hair blond against my objections, and he wore those not acceptable pants to the tournament. I was more concerned with Wally Goodwin seeing him with the dyed hair, so I told him to cover it up with his hat in case a picture was taken that Wally would see might make him wonder. The photo appeared in the *LA Times*, and it did not cover up his hair. So much for trying to hide his "rebellion." The dyed hair was not a problem in his senior year because he had already got the scholarship, but the reader already knows what a struggle that was. I thought it made him look ridiculous.

The biggest problem with Peter's revelations in the article is that Brian was not motivated anymore to play golf. He had already achieved his goal of getting the scholarship to Stanford. The concern was that he had realized his dream and that it was a mystery as to what he needed to do next. He had achieved his goal, and now what did he have to do? I accept the responsibility partly for failing to get him to set those goals. As the reader will see, I had told him to do it in a letter on his way to Stanford, but that was different than sitting down with him and asking him what he wanted to do. He had achieved his goal of getting a scholarship to Stanford, and that was all he cared about. The problem was that he didn't know what the responsibility was for that scholarship. If a player gets one, they must earn it to keep it.

I had expected that he would play excellent collegiate golf when he went off to Stanford. Why shouldn't I hope he would do that? He had a tremendous junior amateur career, so why would I not expect him to do well in his first year at Stanford? After all, as a freshman, Wally Goodwin had promised Brian he would play all eleven collegiate tournaments at Stanford.

What I didn't know at the time was Wally Goodwin had decided to retire. I'm unsure when I learned it, but it was not expected. We learned about it in the spring before the high school championship when the players from Stanford came to our house for dinner because they were playing at a tournament nearby. But it was something we had to deal with, and it did not look good right from the beginning of our knowledge of who was selected.

Brian said at one point in the interview, "It took precedence over everything else." The "It" was getting a scholarship to Stanford. Twenty years later, I looked at it and saw how that was so true. So true that it was more important than anything in the family. The irony of Peter Yoon claiming that we were casual about golf is hogwash. To achieve a goal like that, one must be obsessed with it. As Peter indicates in the article, that is what it was, an obsession. Brian's obsession was made good by the sacrifices of the entire family. We went to Colorado on vacation because that was where he was playing a tournament! He devoted his full summers to playing golf tournaments to improve his performance. I realize that many other families were doing the same to achieve that lofty goal. Often a PGA Tour player will thank his family for all their sacrifices to get them where they arrived. We sacrificed for this goal. More than most people will ever know.

When I taught at Cypress College, part of the course I taught to students who were returning to college after a long absence from school was study skills. One of my lectures was about setting goals. There were daily, weekly, semester, and ultimate goals. I say this because it was a significant omission in my son's life. After all, despite planning to get to Stanford, he did not see beyond that, as we discovered in the interview with Peter Yoon of the *LA Times*. After reading and internalizing the May interview about Brian's thinking, I was worried about what he wanted to do when he got to Stanford, so I drafted the following letter. When I wrote it, I was sure I had no idea what would happen when he went to Stanford.

I wrote the letter because I wanted him to know how much fun it was to have been able to participate in guiding him to his first primary goal in life: getting a scholarship to Stanford. Below is the letter I wrote to him when he was already there in his first week.

A Letter to Brian on His Way to Stanford
"Hit It into The Lights"

"Dad, where do I hit it? I can hardly see the green!"

"That one tall light on the clubhouse is in direct line with the flag. Hit it into the lights behind the green," said Dad.

"Are we still playing for five dollars?" asked Brian.

"Yes! We are even going into this last hole, so you will have to birdie the hole to win." chimed Dad.

"This is fun, Dad—playing in the dark! I can't see the green!

Brian sets up, takes aim, and cracks a nine-iron right into the light behind the green. Dad answered with a slightly pulled wedge shot left of the lights (his back was hurting, so he had to use his arms to hit the shot). Brian grabs his bag and starts running toward the green, anxiously looking to see how he has hit his shot. Brian's ball had come to rest about four or five feet from the pin. Dick had hit his wedge too long and left, about twenty-five feet away. Dick hit his putt first, the ball coming up short as it usually does in the dark. Brian, knowing he needed the putt for five dollars (money makes Brian's eyes grow more prominent), took his time. He smoothly stroked the ball and hit the cup center cut. Dad reluctantly pulls out the five dollars and pays off Brian.

Dear Brian,

There were so many scenes like this over the years we played golf. Brian, I can't remember them all. Throughout the years that we played golf together, the times when you showed great enthusiasm for the game were the best. They were the times we played until it was dark or when we played in the rain. When you were in love with golf, it seemed like time would stop. I remember riding along the cart path of Dove Canyon, singing, "Olazabal, you're swell, but you smell like hell!" There were so many good times at Newport Beach Country Club as well. Today, things have changed, and golf has become the humbling game it is. Like Ron Won, I am glad you learned this lesson early rather than later. I would like to tell you about a few things that golf has done for you, Brian.

First, golf has given you the means to get to Stanford University, the best college in the country. How proud am I of that accomplishment by you? Well, I could not express how happy I am for you that all your hard work in golf has paid off in the form of an outstanding scholarship to Stanford. For accomplishing this, I am immeasurably proud of you. Very few people in this country have accomplished what you have accomplished. You deserve Stanford's excellent education and all the good things that will come to you due to getting a degree from Stanford. Remember that the goal still needs to be quite accomplished. You will have to go up there and work hard again. You will be reading and writing and reading and writing, and you will get one of the best educations a person can get. Don't turn your cheek on any of it. Everything you learn at Stanford will help you at some time in your life—I guarantee it.

I cannot tell you how amazed the people I know are at your accomplishment of getting to Stanford. There are tons and tons of people you have never met who have come up to me and congratulated you on your achievement. All this came because you played golf. You and I know that getting to Stanford through academics is next to impossible! It is just as tough to get there athletically as it is to get there academically. There are more spots for people with good grades than there are for athletes who have good grades and are athletically capable. Therefore, your accomplishment is phenomenal. A couple of guys are coming to Stanford with you, but they are not getting the scholarship you are, making your achievement much more special.

Golf has allowed you to travel. We have been all over the country and have been to Japan three times. These experiences are once in a lifetime. I don't think I'll ever spend my money and go to Japan, but I was happy to see some of that great country. Golf did that for you and us.

Golf gives you a great self-concept. You were told so many times how great it was that you did what you did when you played golf throughout your junior and high school career. You had one of the best high school careers anyone can have. How good is it to be the player of the year for three years and all of Orange County for four years, not to mention the title of CIF Champion in two of the four years? Many players would have loved to win that championship just once! You also have an excellent record in the books—a 65. It may be a long time before that record goes down because it is tough to do that in a one-day tournament. The many things you accomplished in golf made you feel good about yourself.

Golf allows you to keep balance in your life. You worked at your golf, and you worked at your grades. You dedicated yourself to getting to Stanford, and you did it. I could not be happier for you, Brian. It is the reward for all your hard work, and it is a reward for all the colonial times you missed. Recently, I watched an interview with Pete Sampras.

Interestingly, you are so much like him. You have similar personal qualities. When he was young, he did not do anything but play tennis. He was obsessively focused on tennis. He dedicated himself to becoming one of the best players and has accomplished that goal. He is the best. He did not go to a prom. He did not go out. He did not drink or socialize. I'm glad that you did. At least you can reflect on your high school career as a social person and say that you had fun. Yet, there is a price to pay for that. You did not accomplish all of your golf goals. You wanted to be better than you were at the national level, but it required more dedication. It needed more work than you or I wanted you to put in—even though we both wanted you to do better. It was not possible. It took too much time to be good at the grades and too much time to be as good as you were in golf. You have that single-minded focus that is necessary to be great at anything.

Golf gave me some of the best moments of my life with you, Brian. When you won the junior world championship, it was one of the best moments of my life to see you win that championship. When you beat the two high school champion-ships, I don't know which one I was prouder of you for doing. When you played so well in your high school competitions, I just don't know which accomplishment made me fill up with pride for your excellent work. So often, we played late into the evening, and I would tell you to hit it into the lights when you couldn't see the green. It reminded me of Tiger winning that championship in the dark. I don't know a lot of difference in talent between you and Tiger. He was singularly focused like Pete Sampras and had the advantage of better teachers. I believe that you are headed in the right direction with your swing. For all the times we had together on the trips, and the good and the bad, I'll never forget the great opportunity I had to be with you and watch you grow up. I realize I made mistakes along the way, and I am very sorry. I wished I could take back everything I said that wasn't right, but your dad is not perfect. There is no dress rehearsal for being a parent. However, many people are proud of what I did for you, what mom and I sacrificed for you, and the many hours I gave freely of my life for you. It will all be worth it the day you graduate from Stanford, and no matter what you choose to do in life, I will be proud of you.

Golf will be vital to you in your life. You will be asked to show people how well you can play this game, and they will pay you for it with more prominent deals or businesses. They will want to be around you and will want to see you play great golf.

You should have a better attitude about golf. I just pointed out to you what golf has given to you. I know you don't believe in the golf gods (even Tiger uses the phrase), but they are content with someone who is having a good time playing, looks at the game as a challenge, and is positive in their approach to golf. "Let your attitude about golf determine your game, but don't let your attitude be the determiner of your game...." Davis Love's dad said about golf. If you hate golf and don't enjoy playing it, then your attitude is affecting your game, but if you approach it humbly (as you do), with a positive attitude, and enjoy the game (it is only a game and it will not determine life or death issue), you will then go a long way. Laugh, have fun, and don't get upset at your mistakes so much. Try to control how you feel about your mistakes. The better you control your reaction to the misses, the better you'll play. I started double-bogey, bogey, and I still made a target with "The Firm" the other day.

Golf requires a lot of preparation. I realize you have been working hard, but I never knew how badly you must work to be good. You are on the right track. These last two months have been excellent. You worked hard. The results are starting to show, but you must continue to work hard if you expect to improve. You are close enough to hit the ball well. Continue to work hard at Stanford, and you will begin to enjoy the fruits of your labor after a while, and you will begin to enjoy golf again. Just don't give up so easily. You tend to get down too much on the golf course. Don't let a couple of misses get you down.

Keep thinking positive and working hard, and you will get better than you have ever been. I guarantee it. Remember that you don't have to worry about physical problems, so you should be fresh to show the coach a good attitude about golf. He will quickly see who wants to play golf and who likes golf. Speak enthusiastically about golf to Coach Mitchell. He is a man who can help you or get you the help you need. Golf is a combination of the physical game, the mental game, the long game, and the short game. Your short game and mental game need more work than the other two. I would love to see you have a good time up there and play plenty of golf for the team, but you must continue to work hard to improve.

I suggest you listen to David Wright's tapes for the mental game. That may sound ridiculous, but I listened to the recordings four times, and they helped me tremendously. For the course management game, ask Jeff Mitchell to help you with that. You still need to see the course differently. For the long game and your swing, I would probably get someone to work with up there, or you'll have to keep in touch with Don Hill via tapes in the mail. You'll learn from Jeff Mitchell and the other players for the short game. This game is an art; it takes a lot of study and attention to detail. I know you will do well up at Stanford, Brian. You have a lot of support and many people pulling for you.

When you are young and you dream of having a family, you hope that the kids you have will turn out well. I could not be luckier to have two great kids like you and Jennie in ten life-times. I can't tell you how happy you have brought mom and me. I know the road to success was not paved with diamonds. There were many bumps in the road along the way. That's life. Not all things go according to plan, but if I were to write a script of how I would want my kids to turn out, it would be the way you guys are. Thank you for the great memories of your wonderful childhood and adolescence. Now, you are a young man off to college, off on your own, and off to many great adventures. As a dad, I know this is the end of having you around. I hope you will come home to visit one day, and we can talk about your great experiences.

At Stanford, learn to speak up for yourself and communicate well with people. Try not to say anything negative. Try only to say positive things and surround yourself with the best people. I wish you all the best.

Love Always,
Dad

The reader can judge the letter themselves, but from my perspective, twenty years later, it looks like a dad appealing to his son to get out there and play some good golf for Stanford. I am writing this knowing so much more than I did then. I did not see that he was "done" with golf because he had reached his goal. I just assumed that playing there for four years would be part of the deal, part of the responsibility for the scholarship, and partly the promise I had made to Wally to ensure that he got the scholarship. One of the ironies one suffers in life is what happens as opposed to what was supposed to happen.

These are some of the highlights of Brian's senior year.

National Tournaments:

Date	Tournament	Place	Scores	Field	Location	Yardage
6/00	US Open Qualifier	7th	73-72	145	Aliso Niguel GC	6500
8/00	US Am Qualifier	10th	74-71	145	Warner Springs GC	6890

High School:

Date	Tournament	Place	Scores	Field	Location	Yardage
5/00	CIF Team Regionals	1st	71	48	Serrano GC	6800
5/00	CIF Individual Regionals	1st	71	72	Huntington Seacliff	6700

California Interscholastic Federation (CIF) Finals: 7th place
CIF Sectional Qualifying: 1st place (score 71)
Orange County Register: First Team All-Orange County 2000
Los Angeles Times: First Team All-Orange Country 2000
Los Angeles Times: Athlete of the Week
First Team: All-Pacific Coast League 2000
University High School: Most Valuable Player 2000
Medalist Honors: 13 Times in League
School Sports.Com: Player of the Week

Chapter 14: 2001

The Dream Becomes a Nightmare

"My dream has turned into a Nightmare."

Martin Luther King

In the fall of 2000, Brian drove to Stanford and began his career as a player for that university, or so I thought. The first story I heard from Stanford was that Coach Goodwin was still there. I assumed he wanted to say goodbye to the players because he had announced his retirement in the spring. It was a shock to the players that Wally was leaving because he loved being the coach at Stanford. It was rumored that his wife wanted him to retire, and so he did, but I am sure there were more factors in it than that. There was a wonderful celebration with all his past players sometime in the spring of Brian's senior year in high school. And I had indicated our knowledge of that fact when the team came to dinner at our house in the spring because they were playing in a tournament at a course in Coto de Caza, CA.

Two years later, I would learn the team's sentiments during the hiring of the new coach in the spring of 2000.

There were two finalists—one from the University of Minnesota and one from Texas Tech University. Ron Won had indicated to Brian at the dinner at our house that he had hoped that the University of Minnesota coach was selected. Ron also said that he thought they would go with the Texas Tech coach because he was a former PGA Tour player who had won one tournament. Stanford may have wanted to finally put someone who could actually "help" the players instead of a coach who motivates and cannot help them with their swings because of a lack of knowledge. Anyway, an additional factor that I learned was that the women's coach from Stanford was on the selection committee, and she knew the Texas Tech coach and thought he would be significant for the program. When the team was asked to vote for which of the two coaches they wanted, they gave nine of ten votes to the University of Minnesota coach.

In Brian's notes that he would send to me in his junior year, he said, "They hired a new coach for my freshman year, and it made me nervous because I had had some tough experiences with coaches in the past." Brian was referring to his first three years at University High School, where he had a freshman football coach as his golf coach. The coach, Craig Huff, screamed and yelled at the players and scared them to death because he thought their behavior was unacceptable. As we know, Brian did not make friends with him because, despite winning the CIF Championship his freshman year, the coach gave him The Most Improved Player Award. Essentially it was a slap in the face. He was easily the co-player of the year at worst. I assume the coach did not like Brian, and I have already told that story.

The Texas Tech coach was hired, much to the team's objection, and the four years with him were already off to a bad start. It was learned that the new coach was coming from Texas Tech, where he had been the women's coach for the last ten years. Even though he had been the women's coach from Texas Tech, he had some excellent credentials as a former player and winner on the PGA Tour. Naturally, one would assume that he had great expertise in golf, but that isn't the issue at this point in the narrative.

Brian told me that the team's first round of practice was at least two or three weeks ahead of the beginning of school. When he got on the first tee, Wally Goodwin, standing alongside Coach Jeff Mitchell, said, "Coach Mitchell, here is your next NCAA Individual Champion from Stanford." Brian told me he looked at Wally and wondered WHY he said that. In other words, Wally had expected Brian to continue to make gains in his golf game and be capable of winning that prestigious championship before he finished with Stanford. Remember, this is the man who coached Tiger Woods, so Wally believed that Brian had that capability. Wally again said he would play Brian in all eleven tournaments in his first year. Brian was quite aware of that fact. Wally Goodwin then disappeared into the sunset and went to Wyoming to retire. We were left wondering what the style and approach Jeff Mitchell would make for the young men playing for Stanford.

As the fall season played out, it came and went without Brian playing in any of the five tournaments the team had scheduled. I was beside myself at home, wondering what was happening at Stanford. My nightmare had begun. It would take me a while to find out because neither Brian nor my wife shared any information. I would learn that Brian was "injured" and had to spend a lot of time getting therapy for his neck injury.

The reader may recall that in the spring of his senior year in high school, Brian was going to a friend's house as a passenger in the car. His friend stopped to make a left turn on a one-lane highway, and the car behind them did not see that fact and hit the back end of the vehicle on the right-hand side. Brian's neck was injured. We had a friend at Newport Beach Country Club who was a personal injury lawyer, and he offered to take Brian's case and file a claim. Brian won the lawsuit sometime in his freshman year of college, but when he got to Stanford, Brian told the coach he was having problems with his neck and needed therapy. I assume that is why he never qualified for any tournament in the fall. He was injured and could not perform. In the meantime, Dad was having a stroke and was beside himself, because he was expecting his son to play for the team right away!

Although he did not qualify for the regular team tournament called The Prestige held at Desert Willow Golf Course in Palm Desert, CA, the coach sent him to a tournament along with several other "B" squad players to the Dusty Destruel Invitational. There the JV Team finished third in the tournament of ten teams. More importantly, Brain scored second among the sixty players on the field. The unfortunate thing about that was that the coach never said anything to him about how he did, and he acted like it didn't even happen. I would assume that any player needs their coach's approval, and coach Mitchell did not think it was anything.

More importantly, the coach didn't know the winning background of Brian's golf game before coming to Stanford. I guess, again, that he did not care and would measure the players by his standards. After all, he had played on the PGA Tour, so he surely knew what he was talking about! But the fall season finished after that tournament, and it would not be until late January of the following year before another tournament. I know that in the meantime, Brian had learned that Dad was not exactly happy about the events that occurred in the fall. I did not say a thing to him about that fall season, but I assume his mother did.

I don't remember him coming home for the holidays because it was always about schoolwork. Stanford was on the quarter system, so there was an autumn quarter from September to mid-December, a winter quarter from January to March, and a spring quarter from April to June. The players had to negotiate their golf work around those quarters.

The winter quarter had started, and the players were back at school for the six tournaments in the winter and spring before they would play the Pac-10 Championships, the Western Regionals, and then the NCAA Finals for golf. The first tournament in the winter was the Ping Arizona Intercollegiate. In the qualifying round, Brain finished fifth. The coach took seven guys, but Brian was not one of them. According to the notes I received from Brian in his junior year, he said, "One of the trends he (Coach Mitchell) started here, it seemed, was him not sticking to his word. In this case, he told us that if a freshman scored the same as upperclassmen on the Stanford golf course, they would have a preference in being selected for tournaments since they haven't had nearly as much experience on the Stanford golf course." Brian considered that since the coach did not select him to play, he had violated the very "rule" he had announced to players earlier.

Brian said he went to the coach's office and argued his case. The coach had no honest response but simply indicated that his decision about the team was final. A month later, there was another qualifying one-day tournament at the Stanford course. For this tournament, the coach was only taking five players, perhaps because of the travel expense. Again, according to

Brian, he had finished low enough in the qualifying to be chosen for the tournament. As a freshman, he had qualified in the top five, but again, he was left off the team. It was the John Burns Intercollegiate at Leilehua Golf Course in Honolulu, Hawaii. There were nineteen teams at the tournament, and Stanford finished fifth in the tournament, with two players of the five not doing well.

When he went to the coach's office to look for his name on the traveling list, it was not there. He was upset and confused. The coach had indicated that the first three players who qualified were automatically on the traveling team. Then the next four were at the discretion of the coach despite saying that any freshman who qualified in the top five would travel with the team because they hadn't had as much experience playing the course at Stanford, so they would be highly considered. He wasn't, as I would learn not too long after this incident. I encouraged him to ask the coach why he was not playing, and he did. I am unsure what the coach told him, but it did not end well.

I assume the problems began almost from the get-go. Brian had anticipated a regime that allowed him to schedule his practices and only be required to attend qualifying tournaments and team meetings. He would not have long discussions on the range with a coach endlessly talking about how to hit a golf ball. Brian loved playing golf for Stanford because he could schedule his practices as Wally Goodwin had told him when he was recruited. With Coach Mitchell, this was not the case. Although I do not know exactly how he set up the schedule for the players but whatever it was, it was not liked by the players. This was different from what Brian had expected. His belief that he would operate under one system was quickly dispelled by a coach who wanted to use his design. Brian said he went to Stanford with his best attitude despite this knowledge. It didn't matter.

The new coach had set up his system of "coaching" the players. He also set up the "rules" by which a player could qualify for the traveling team. That team consisted of seven players, five of which would play for the Stanford team and two of which would go to gain experience playing in a college tournament. The college golf season is divided into two seasons: the fall season and the spring season, so it is pretty challenging for players attending a college of this academic stature and always playing their sport. There are usually four tournaments in the fall and six tournaments in the spring. Then come the PAC-12 Championships, the Regionals, and the NCAA Championships. It can be a challenging schedule to handle one's academics if one is playing in all of these tournaments. Stanford has the right major for players to ease the pressure. Brian was encouraged to major in economics.

During the fall of 2000, as each tournament came and went, I saw that Brian was not selected to play on the team. I was upset. Wally told me he would play all eleven tournaments in his freshman year. The first two or three tournaments had gone, and I had yet to learn what was going on. Brian would not talk to me, knowing I would be distraught at his not playing for the team. At the time, I thought he would be playing, not sitting on the bench. Did the coach know the level of player that he was? What was going on? Why wasn't he playing? At the same time, he was calling his mother, explaining what was going on and why he was not playing. I did not get accurate information from either of them.

I finally talked with Brian, who explained that he was overlooked twice for the traveling team. "Why?" I asked. He explained that the coach had set up specific rules for qualifying.

If a player was in the top three during the qualifying round, they would automatically go to the tournament. If they finished in the top five, they would be considered an excellent choice to go with the traveling team. "Especially," the coach said, "if the player was a freshman because they had not had the advantage of playing the Stanford Golf Course like their older classmates." According to Brian, he qualified in the top five twice, and he was overlooked for the traveling team both times.

My conversation with Brian on the phone that night was an hour or so, and he sounded like a defeated player. Imagine never having to worry about playing for the team for several years in high school, being told that he would play all eleven tournaments in his freshman year, and finally, getting rejected by the coach after "qualifying" twice. It was more than he could handle.

After being rejected the first time, he went to see the coach in his office, and the coach said, "Sorry, the team has been set." When it happened a second time, and again Brian made his appeal to the coach; he said to him, "The decisions have been made, and they are final." Imagine that. Imagine expecting one thing and getting the opposite. Imagine thinking he would play eleven tournaments in his freshman year, and he found himself begging the coach to let him play. A few weeks later, he did not qualify for the next tournament, and he was sent to another secondary tournament as the Stanford "B" squad. It was a tournament in Santa Clara, and Brian finished in second place. According to Brian, the coach never said anything about his performance.

His behavior led me to conclude that the coach did not care for Brian and his attitude. How a coach can be so punitive to a player who came with his credentials is beyond comprehension.

The fall season passed, and nothing came from the last two tournaments. I was despondent. I was beside myself because it was to be the greatest joy for me to know that my son was playing for the Stanford golf team, regardless of how he did! I understood that he would be playing all eleven tournaments, the entire fall season had passed, and he played the one tournament with the coach saying nothing to him about his performance. As I look back on this twenty years later, his performance in that tournament would have been the same in any tournament if the coach had just shown confidence in him as a player. Then a bizarre thing happened.

The coach emailed me in the spring before the tournaments started and asked me for a resume of Brian's golf accomplishments. What? I could not believe it. I was doubtful about why he asked me for something that I thought he already knew because we filled out a bio for Brian for his team for the publications at Stanford. This was not enough for the coach, so he had more information about his performances. It took me hours and hours to show him all of Brian's tournaments and accomplishments and get them all on a resume. When I sent it to the coach, he did not respond or say thanks or anything. I was not feeling excellent about this guy, and it was not headed in the right direction.

Brian felt the year could be salvaged, so after the coach returned from Hawaii with the team, Brian asked the coach for a red shirt year. The coach agreed that this would be good, and he promised to act on his behalf to get that done. The problem was that it had to be a medical red shirt due to an injury that Brian suffered playing golf at Stanford. The coach was sure that he could get that done. Brian wrote, "For the rest of the year, the coach told me that he was confident in my getting a red shirt, so I did not try to compete in the second half of the year. In the end, I realized that I never even had a chance at a medical red shirt because I was injured (my main injury) before coming to Stanford. This caused some embarrassment for Susan Burke and Jeff Mitchell since they had indicated their confidence in my getting my red shirt. In fact, they felt they needed to compensate me for my loss of a year of eligibility–both of them promised my dad and me (Jeff promised me, Susan promised my dad) that I would receive financial aid from the athletic department equal to my current scholarship. In essence, I would get the same amount of money I would have received from a red shirt."

I have to admit that I did not realize that this was promised to me and what is a verbal promise if it is not in writing? I missed the chance to ask the committee for the red-shirt year that Brian was promised but did not qualify for. It was their error saying he could get it. Then we had to pay for his senior year when they were responsible for taking away a year because the coach and his administrative assistant were incompetent.

Brian's final message about the freshmen year was quite disturbing: "Among other grievances, Alex Aragon, a senior, was always battling with coach Mitchell (Alex made it to the PGA Tour but did not do well overall). However, the other player who made a statement that summarized the feelings of the team was when Jimmy Lee, a senior like Alex, said to the coach at one of the final meetings of the year that 'he didn't think the coach cared about the team at all' and he listed several reasons why that was. He also said that he would like for the coach to 'stay out of his way and he'd do the same.' This shocking event indicated early universal discontent on the Stanford men's golf team. Many of us had and still have the same opinion about Coach Mitchell. Simply, he is not here for us, he doesn't care how we do, and he is not a leader and certainly not a coach."

Remember, Brian is writing this in retrospect of his first three years on the golf team at Stanford.

Brian indicated his discontent with Stanford Golf was rising, but he wanted to play. Brian learned how important fulfilling his obligation as a player at Stanford was. He got a scholarship to perform and not sit and watch the world go by.

A parent or parents can put all this energy into getting their kid to achieve a childhood dream, which a bad coach can destroy. During this challenging time, all of my friends at Newport Beach Country Club who supported Brian were wondering how he was doing. All I could tell them was that he was having a difficult time with the new coach, that Wally Goodwin had retired before Brian got there, and the six years of planning to play for Wally at Stanford went up in smoke. The club pro, Paul Hahn, told me after hearing my story, "Dick, that kind of crap goes on all the time at the college level. It happened to us at San Jose State. It is a shame that Brian has to go through something like that. He was a wonderful player."

Brain claimed that his discontent with Stanford golf was rising, but he still wanted to play.

Chapter 15: 2002

The Nightmare Continues

"If you expect nothing from somebody,
you are never disappointed."

Sylvia Plath, *The Bell Jar*

To my knowledge, Brian's sophomore year was worse than his freshman year because he didn't qualify for a tournament. He didn't qualify for any tournaments, so he was not invited to attend them. He managed to play in two tournaments, both of which took place at Stanford. Stanford holds two tournaments a year at their university course, and it is a treat for any college player to play there because the course is impressive. Stanford golf course was the course that Tiger Woods played on, and they all wanted to challenge it.

Five tournaments were to be played in the fall of Brian's sophomore year, and he was not chosen to play in the first three. The fourth tournament of the autumn quarter takes place at Stanford. Because Stanford was hosting this tournament, it was a long way into the fall season.

Collegiate tournaments are three-day events, with five players on each team. The top four scores are counted for the team against each other, but all scores count for the individual championship. Being the medalist at these tournaments is a big deal, indicating that the player may be capable of more significant competition. At this tournament, because it's at the team's home base, they can play the regular team, and other players can compete for the individual title. Well, not really. They would be on the team and not playing individually if they played well. I learned that Brian finished last in this tournament with scores of 82-84-82 with a total of 248 or 35 over par. This tells me that he was not prepared to play, was not practiced, and was not into playing. The coach gave him a chance to play and said, "See, he is incapable." This was nonsense. Brian's kind of record as a junior did not change his ability. He could play well, but he no longer wanted to play well, especially for that coach. His notes for that year were brief, and I'm sure he didn't want me to know that he misplayed this. I was still hoping he would somehow be discovered as the player he was on his way to Stanford.

The second tournament, which was at Stanford, was called the U.S. Collegiate. It was played on April 20th and 21st. He finished last in the tournament with 79-80-78 or 237.

I was worried about his obligation because I was reflecting on when Wally Goodwin asked me if he would continue to work hard when he came to Stanford and I told the coach he would. It was a natural question to ask, and I did not think anything of it other than he needed to perform to the level of his ability. When tournament after tournament came and went, and I did not see any performance from Brian, I wrote him the following letter.

Dear Brian,

March 9, 2001

Throughout the years that you learned to play golf, I never talked about when you became a pro golfer or had the intention that you become a pro golfer. Now, did I want you to be a pro golfer? Well, every father's dream is to have his kid become a professional athlete, whether a football player, a basketball player, or a hockey player. But I know this is the father's dream for his kid to be such a thing, and it is not the kid's dream. I learned a long time ago that your heart was not in this has turned out to be a challenging year on the golf team. There may be several causes: your back and neck, lack of adequate preparation before going to Stanford, or the time spent doing anything else. What happened to the effort to go to the gym and make yourself physically strong?

I know the answer to that question. Once you achieved the goal of getting to Stanford, you had no more goals. Some people operate well with dreams, and you need to work well with some golf plans.

I have another question. Do you get a scholarship for what you performed before you got to Stanford, or is the scholarship given for what you do while at Stanford? Is Casey Jacobson getting his scholarship for his past high school performance, or is he getting it for showing up to practice, busting his butt, and performing on the basketball court? I am still determining what it is for. Let me give you some evidence: when you came home for Christmas break, it was more important to go out with your friends and party than to get up and spend a few hours preparing for the competition upon returning to Stanford. Yes, I recognize that you did well when you and the coach didn't pick you, but what if you had finished one place higher? I don't know why the coach didn't choose you, because I haven't talked to him about it. Are you not an athlete at Stanford who owes them a better effort than you are?

Here is your answer: You are getting the scholarship for the time and effort that you put into the athletic program while you are there. I want to be sure that you own up to that responsibility. You owe them the best effort you can make, not staying up until 2:30 in the morning and not drinking during the season. If it is off-season, I don't care if you drink. If you regularly drink during the season, you are not making your best effort for the Stanford athletic department. You are responsible for doing your best and improving your mental, physical, and skill performances. That is why you are getting thousands of dollars to attend Stanford. I don't care how you do. I can see how much of an effort you make.

Perhaps you've been caught in a bind. You can't perform both the academic and the athletic requirements. You probably have a tough time because you have not learned how to manage your time well. Not as good as you think. You have often told me on the phone, "you don't know how they do that." You don't know how an athlete gets his academics done and job on the field. Well, you have to learn better time management. I can see from the time we spent up there that you don't use it effectively. You can go to other athletic events but don't have time to spend an hour at the range working for your scholarship. That Sunday, I doubt you went to the golf course and worked on the game. I understand that you probably planned to get the red shirt and weren't motivated to work on the game. However, there is no guarantee that you are going to get it. I know the coach may be behind it, but I don't understand why you would not be getting prepared for the next qualifying.

When mom and I left you off at Stanford, we were hopeful that things would go well for you. We both cried when we drove down the street because we knew that would be the end of our control over you. Well, it isn't. You owe us some respect if we work hard to pay the additional money to put you through Stanford. The car you were given to use at Stanford was supposed to be an incentive to do well athletically. It has not done that. I realize you have excuses for not doing well, but some are not very good. That car is an extraordinary gift for a college freshman, and there have been times when I do not think you deserve it. Why? For one simple reason, and that is that you believe that Stanford owes you the scholarship, but instead, you need to earn it. You need to pay them back with performance. You need to contribute to their great athletic program. That is why you are there. They didn't give you an academic scholarship.

You should do well academically. I want you to put in whatever effort you can, and I want you to do well. However, I also want you to contribute to the athletic program of Stanford to repay them for the outstanding scholarship that you got. I could care less if you became a pro. I know you don't want to anyway, and that is okay with me, but what is not okay is not contributing to the athletic program at Stanford, so I can be proud of what you contributed to that program. I don't care if you finish in the middle of the pact in every tournament you play in! You don't want to be a pro, which is your choice. Do I think it is a wise choice? I don't think it is an intelligent choice, but that is just what I believe, and I know what you think of what I think.

Here are some reasons why you should not give up on golf. You are going to live to be over one hundred years old. The average age span of people today has grown to seventy-four for men and seventy-nine for women. In 2020, the average age span will jump seven more years to eighty-one and eighty-six. That's my generation. I'm supposed to live to be eighty-one, at the least! Add to this mix that grandpa is eighty-six, and you have a lot of good genes working for you. You will easily live to be one hundred years old. Imagine you finish school at twenty-two and work for a company or whatever. If you work thirty-eight years at whatever, you will only be sixty years old when you "retire" from that job. You will still have forty years to go, and many will be good years. You don't, in other words, need to start your life at a company at age twenty-two. You can try to make a living at golf until you are thirty and still have a ton of time to make money. You will meet many people who will give you your dream job, too, instead of letting somebody snatch you up from Stanford and get you behind a desk for forty years. You can say that what I am saying is a bunch of bunk, but just ask anybody in my generation what they would do in your shoes. It doesn't have to be Jim Okuley or any of the players in The Firm but ask anyone over forty years old. I dare you.

Now, I feel better just for saying what I should have said long ago. I am a terrible communicator, Brian. You aren't excellent, either. You mumble, and you hardly have anything to say. Maybe you are afraid to tell me that you don't like golf and you don't want to have anything to do with it. I would respect you more if you said to me that than to go sneaking around and ducking your responsibilities. If you find golf repulsive, then why don't you hand back the scholarship, and we will find a way to get you through Stanford without the burden of having to do golf? By the way, you have approached golf this year, and this looks like the direction you are headed. You can say all you want about your back and stuff like that, but I think you can tell the difference between you and Travis Whisman. He has a herniated disk (super painful), and somehow, he has been able to perform this year—end of the story about your back. If you were motivated, you would find a way to play. I know you are not, so you don't work to find a way to get into the lineup.

If the coach gets you a red shirt, you have one more opportunity to make him want you as a player. You need to take advantage of the opportunity and not squander everyday opportunities to improve your game. I repeat. I want you to be something other than a pro, but anyone with your talent should at least try it. You will not regret just trying. What you will regret is that you didn't even try. You'll see guys with less talent than you who you golfed with your whole life making tons of money, and you'll be drinking a beer in the bar and saying, "why didn't I do that?" It's just like Steven Sinay, who beat the Sutherlands when he was a kid, but they worked their way up from the California tour to the Nike tour to the PGA. They both have made a great living.

Your degree from Stanford is enhanced immensely if you take a promising career in golf along with it. Even if you never decide to go at the tour, a promising career as a golf player at Stanford is worth tons more than just a degree from Stanford.

Every day is an opportunity to make yourself a better player. Are you going to take the challenge and make yourself better to fulfill your obligation to the Stanford athletic department for giving you this wonderful scholarship gift?

When you come home, I want some answers. I want you to tell me what your goals are and what you plan to do to accomplish them. I want you to decide to accomplish whatever you wish at Stanford. I don't care if it is just to play in ten tournaments, but you need to set some new goals. If you're going to drop golf, start thinking of how to earn money to pay for your education. I am not expecting you to decide what your goals are beyond college. I want you to try to be a pro, and if you don't make it, then at least you can say when you are old that you tried. Anybody who has a single scoring record better than Tiger Woods has to try at least to play golf for a living. If you decide not to try, don't come to me when you are thirty-five or forty and say I'm sorry I didn't try. If you try and fail, I'll be a happy man. If you don't try and give up before you even try, I will have a hard time respecting that. You have been given a gift, a talent that not many people get. Please don't throw it away before you get a chance to exercise it.

I want nothing but the best for you, and I want you to be honest. I don't want you to be circumventing your duty at Stanford.

Love,
Dad

This was a pretty dumb letter when I begged him to try professional golf when he did not even want to play for his college team. Well, that isn't entirely fair, but it seems apparent that he was no longer interested in performing for this coach or in golf. I was struggling to find the reasons for Brian to make more of an effort to play, but by this time, it was already too late to change his thinking. He had gone to Stanford with the idea of playing, but he got turned down, and in turn, he turned down the coach. The coach had enough of it, as we will see in the next year of play.

All this reflection has taught me that, looking back on this,

Chapter 15: 2002

I can see what happened clearly. The first thing that comes to mind is that the coach never knew Brian's golf record. He never took the time to see that Brian was a perfect player, but many of the people at Newport Country Club thought he would be a pro. A pro played out of Newport on the Senior Tour by the name of Esteban Toledo. He had told Brian that if he continued to improve, playing on the PGA Tour would be easy. Esteban was quite impressed with Brian's golf skills. It wasn't that he couldn't play at a high level, the desire was gone, and he was just going through the motions for the coach.

Brian had turned his attention to more academic life at Stanford when he found the major, he wanted to pursue: symbolic systems. I can't describe to you what this major is, so I will not do so except to say that it is a second cousin to a computer science degree. It is a challenging major and requires a lot of time for anyone to accomplish. I was curious when Brian started the work for this major, but the usual is to start the work in the junior year. The academic work for the sophomore year is pretty rugged, so there's never any let-up for the players. The last two years can be more accessible if the player chooses to do a more accessible degree; some are a lot easier than others.

It was recommended that golf players get a degree in economics. Wally Goodwin suggested this to Brian on our tour of the campus. I do know that Brian was living with students in his dorm who were computer science majors, so they influenced his willingness to go for anything like that. I met several of those fine young men, and they were all funny and intelligent. Brian picked a great bunch of friends at Stanford. It appears that they were not golfers. He never hung out with them, as far as I know.

The end of sophomore year came, Brian came home, and it was not a pleasant situation. I was not privy to all the information I gathered for this memoir then, and he kept information from me, like his two performances in his sophomore year. I knew he was not trying anymore, and it bothered me, so I said something about it. He got mad as hell at me and threw his water bottle against the wall. He was incapable of explaining what was going on so I could understand how anyone with the kind of talent he had could not even play one tournament for the team at Stanford! He would explain nothing to me and walk away, and we did not talk about it until the fall of his junior year.

In the media guide for the 2001-2002 season, Brian was listed as having had a red shirt in his freshman year. It does not show results for competition in his freshman year. He did play, but Coach Jeff Mitchell never recognized it. Despite the claim that he would get a red shirt for the loss of his freshman year, it never materialized. I was lied to just as Brian was by his coach. The nasty aspect of this man was getting on my nerves, but there was nothing to do about it

Chapter 16: 2003

Getting Blindsided by Coach Mitchell

"You never really understand a person until you consider things from his point of view. Until you climb inside of his skin and walk around in it."

Atticus Finch in *To Kill a Mockingbird*

By the fall of 2002, Brian's junior year, he had nothing going in the way of golf. The first three tournaments had gone, and I figured he would never play for Stanford. I was right. I wrote this letter to the Athletic Directors about Brian's experiences as a player for Stanford. I wanted them to know that this coach should not be coaching Stanford kids. He was the wrong choice. The players have already said that in their meetings with the coach so the coach had to find a scapegoat for all his troubles, and Brian was a good target. . I wrote this letter to the Athletic Directors asking for help in allowing Brian to play golf at Stanford. I still had expectations.

October 14, 2002

Dear Dr. Leland and Mr. Schuhmann,

I am writing this letter because it is necessary to explain why my son, Brian Sinay, has difficulty in the golf program at Stanford University.

When Brian was finishing his senior year in high school, he tried to tie an incredible record held by Tiger Wood to win the Southern Section (580 high schools) individual championship three times. Brian did not win the championship in his senior year, but he did place in the top ten, and with a few bounces, he could have won his third title. He shot 70, a two-under-par performance and the winner shot 67, so he was not far off.

At the end of his senior year, he played confidently and felt good about his game. He had a good summer playing tournaments and was successful in several of them.

Then he arrived at Stanford, full of hope. Wally Goodwin had promised him eleven tournaments in his freshmen year. Although he started poorly in the fall, he regained his form by the spring. I played with him on a challenging course in Hawaii in December, and he shot under par. That spring, he qualified for two tournaments, but Coach Mitchell did not allow him to attend either. Brian Sinay had never been told that he was not good enough to play golf. That was the end of Brian Sinay. His confidence was shattered, and he never regained his form that spring. He requested a red shirt for the golf season because he wanted to play for four years at Stanford. Then someone messed up that red shirt, and he lost his year of eligibility. This was another blow to his confidence.

After speaking with Coach Mitchell, he told me that he would allow Brian to play in the fall of his sophomore year and let him play as a sixth man even if he did not qualify for the tournaments. Well, the coach never gave him that opportunity. He allowed him to play in the one tournament at Stanford as an individual player, not a team player: The Nelson. Brian's confidence was now at an all-time low, and he was very dissatisfied with the inability of the coach to show any confidence in him as a player.

There are several reasons why Brian has not been able to perform for Stanford.

1. The first question is, was it Brian's fault for not overcoming the coach's mistakes? He had some insurmountable objects in his way, and here are just a few of them.

2. Despite an outstanding junior career, he was never given the respect due him when he arrived at Stanford. I discovered that the coach did not know Brian's junior record until I sent it to him in February of his freshman year. Why is it that a coach only has ten players and cannot know their accomplishments in their junior career?

3. Despite asking over and over if Brian would be granted a red shirt in his freshman year, Brian lost the year because someone needed to take the time to check out the details. I believe this is the coach's responsibility.

4. Despite being told that Brian would be playing in tournaments during his sophomore year, he ended up playing nothing except as an individual at the home Stanford tournaments.

5. Despite being told he would help Brian improve his game; he has given Brian very little time.

6. Despite qualifying for tournaments, Brian has been denied the opportunity to play at all.

7. He never turned to Brian and encouraged him to help.

How can a kid perform if he's never allowed to perform? The coach might say Brian has to earn his way on the traveling team, and Brian made it to the top five and then was turned down. How is a player supposed to maintain his confidence?

8. Despite coming to Stanford with excellent credentials, the coach never considered him a possible player. The coach thought Brian was a "political" pull-in, as he referred to some players to me in his office the day Brian showed up to play at Stanford. The coach told me there would be no more "political" pull-ins now that he was the coach. I suppose that he thought Brian was one of those. Wally Goodwin followed Brian's career for six years and did not pick him because he was a "political" pull-in. (Speaking of that, there isn't anyone that does not know how Coach Mitchell got his job).

9. Despite working with the summer golf program, the entire summer and working on his game up there, Coach Mitchell did not give him one bit of help on his game. The coach called me and told me what a fantastic kid Brian was! Did he mean he didn't take the time to find that out in his freshman year?

My wife and I worked very hard to get Brian Sinay to Stanford. For him and us, it was a dream that came true. Because of a non-caring coach, the dream has turned into a nightmare.

Sincerely,
Dick and Heidi Sinay

The first thing I want to share here are the notes that Brian sent me for the hearing that was to take place late in the spring of

2003. I had to step into his shoes to understand what had gone on. I do not remember the exact time, but I know the hearing was toward the end of the school year. I didn't even know what the meeting was about, but it was an appeal made by Brian not to have his scholarship taken away. It was an appeal to keep his scholarship for his senior year!

Brian sent me the notes so I could draft a letter and organize Brian's thinking so that the committee would not agree with the coach's decision to rescind Brian's scholarship. I am sharing the notes about his junior year and have already shared what he said about the previous two years. What he was doing was trying to make a case for the "non-performance" or "bad performance" of the coach.

I did not keep a copy of the letter I sent to Brian to relay to the committee, but it was based on all of the issues Brian felt were wrong with this coach. This was the end of the third year for Coach Mitchell, and apparently, he had one more year on his contract because he coached the team in the 2003-2004 season. These are Brian's notes as he sent them to me. I did not change any words but did an edit for publication.

Brian's Notes
2002 – 2003 Junior Year

"- This was the worst year yet, and many players have and will complain about it. The coaching by Jeff Mitchell was awful.

- In October, the coach called me into his office for a meeting. Little did I know, it would be more like a police interrogation than a meeting. He told me that I was too focused on school and that 'I needed to choose between school and golf.' While this may seem surprising, it is one hundred percent true, and

DJ Powers, our assistant coach, was in the office when he said it. This statement nearly caused me to walk out of the Stanford golf program forever. Never in my wildest, most contrived dreams could I have imagined a statement like that from a STANFORD COACH! Even more disheartening was that he meant it. He even told me to come back to him when I made my decision. I was so upset that I emailed Susan Burke to ask her what I should do. She gave me ideas on how to deal with the situation. This particular situation was never resolved, but it left a very sour taste (even more than I already had) in my mouth about Stanford golf— namely, Jeff Mitchell. The frustrating thing about this meeting was that the coach meant it—it was not really that much of a surprise to me because I knew he did not value education at all. He has no idea what Stanford demands of students academically, and his actions always showed that.

After a dismal autumn season, Del DeWindt shocked everybody and quit the team. The reason why everybody was so surprised was that none of us ever thought Del would quit. He was an outstanding high school athlete who was the last guy you would expect to quit. Del's grievances are numerous, but I can and will elaborate on them if necessary. Among them, the coach told Del that he was "born with a silver spoon in his ass" (of course, the expression is supposed to be "born with a silver spoon in your mouth"). Still, regardless, this is a great example of the lack of respect the coach showed Del. Comments like those, especially given Del's intentions during the meeting, are simply inappropriate.

- At the beginning of the winter quarter, my neck was bothering me, so I went to get therapy in the training room. I did make the mistake of not telling the assistant coach about it

(Coach Mitchell was not there at the time – I forgot why, though) right away but assumed it would be ok since I was injured. Little did I know, I would never return. Coach promptly suspended me for not coming to practice – I was injured, and he never revoked my suspension for the rest of the year. I was badgered off the Stanford golf team...many people I talked to say that they see me getting abandoned by the coach due to my performance."

My argument:

"My dad and I were promised a year paid for by the Stanford Athletic department due to my loss of eligibility freshman year. While the promise was supposed to be for my fifth year, I don't think I will return to play for Coach Mitchell, so my fourth will be my last year at Stanford. Coach Mitchell badgered me off the Stanford golf team. His lack of coaching and leadership abilities has led to poor performances by the team—me included—since he got to Stanford. I believe that the team cannot be successful with him as the coach.

The promise of a fifth year prompted me to take on a more difficult major, one that I will struggle to finish in less than three quarters from now. My parents have been generous enough to cover thirty percent of my education for four years. Thus, I will have a challenging and expensive senior year without the help of the Stanford Athletic Department. I believe I fully deserve the seventy percent scholarship I have been getting – only now, as was promised, it should come from the Athletic department, not the scholarship fund. Any other way seems to me to be nothing more than a broken promise made to my dad and me".

Discovering that my son had been suspended from the Stanford golf program broke my heart. I learned that Brian had been suspended early in the second quarter of his junior year. We knew that earlier in the year, the coach had called him in and asked him to choose between his golf and his school. When Brian had an answer to that question, he was to come to the coach and tell him what he had decided. It was the coach thinking that Brian was more devoted to schooling than to his golf. Did the coach believe that the two times Brian qualified for the team and didn't allow him to play was too much devotion to school and not golf? The coach had already disregarded him for two years, so why would Brian be devoted to his golf in his junior year?

I didn't know if the suspension was permanent or what it entailed, but I learned somehow from another player that it was permanent. I did not have that knowledge from Brian when it happened in his junior year because I think he was afraid to tell me. I learned about this potential loss of his scholarship in the winter quarter of 2003. It was a little time before the actual hearing was to take place. Brian may also have been trying to protect my feelings as he knew how difficult it was for me not to see him participate on the golf team. So together we drafted the argument for him to keep his scholarship and sent it to the committee. The committee would read the views from the coach and Brian and then have a hearing where both could make their appeals to the committee about the suspension of the scholarship.

We went to the meeting, and outside the door were Coach Mitchell and the assistant athletic director Mr. Schuhmann. The coach turned to Brian and me and said, "I am sorry about this," and then he extended his hand. I didn't reach out and simply turned away not even to recognize what he said or that he had opened his hand. This was no damn time for handshaking. Why would I want to shake your hand, Coach Mitchell? We went into the room, and the foreman of the committee laid down the rules. Coach gave his speech, and Brian made his speech.

While the coach talked, we thought he was inarticulate and incapable of making a good argument. Brian then had his chance to speak, and he laid out his complaints about the coach and that the coach never gave him a chance to prove that he was a good player. I thought that Brian's comments were good and well-articulated. They did not ask me to speak, but I nodded in approval to what Brian was saying because this was a case of a new coach coming to the great Stanford University and not knowing what the hell he was doing. How does a coach not know the biographies of the players after a year of being with them?

At the end of the meeting, the foreman said that the committee would review the letters submitted and forward the decision to both the coach and Brian. When we were leaving, one of the committee members, the admissions lady who had admitted Brian to Stanford based on his academic record after being awarded the scholarship, came over to me and said, "It is so gratifying to see that Brian has such a supportive father. I hope his other experiences at Stanford will be better than what happened to his golf." I told her, "Thank you for saying that. I appreciate it." I nearly broke down, but I pulled myself together and tried to smile. She said goodbye and walked away. I just thought how incredibly kind it was for her to say that because she could see how torn I was from attending a meeting of this nature when I had all these expectations about my son going to play golf at Stanford. I could not find her name in my research.

I left Brian, went home, and told my wife that this was over and there was no more to worry about whether Brian would play golf at Stanford. And then I just tried to forget about it until I rediscovered his notes five months ago. That was the end of his junior year at Stanford, and he was no longer a golf team member.

The nightmare was over.

Chapter 17: 2004

No Man's Land

"Nothing will come of Nothing."

King Lear

There was no senior year in golf. Brian's Stanford golf career ended near the middle of his junior year. By the end of his sophomore year, I had given up hope of him ever playing on the team at Stanford. It did not appear anything was coming from nothing. It was a challenging time for me and one that permeated the household. My wife was not as understanding of my pain as I expected because she did not devote one minute to bringing him up to get a golf scholarship to Stanford. I do not think she knew the depth of my pain, and so I had to seek outside counseling to deal with it.

The psychologist did not know the whole story because I did not know the entire story. He told me it was Brian's choice not to play golf for Stanford. He was right about that, but he neglected to think about the obligation a player has to a university when they give an athletic scholarship to a player. It's a contract. They will provide you with room and board and tuition, and you, the player, will perform for them athletically. I tried to tell Brian in my letter near the end of his sophomore year, but it fell on deaf ears or was already over in his head. I wanted him to fulfill his obligation and be able to go to Stanford and get that education. It was also because I had promised Wally that Brian would continue to work hard when he got there. I was also thinking of myself because I wanted to say to people that my son played golf for the Stanford team. I don't believe this was selfish, just what I expected. It was not what I got. Expectation and reality are two different things.

At the same time, Brian ran into obstacles out of his control. He could not circumvent the coach's choices about him playing for the team and made those choices based on what he felt was right. I disagree with how he handled my son, but it was nothing I could control.

The senior year was quiet, and there was very little coming from there in communication. We left Brian alone to concentrate on finishing his degree in symbolic systems. I didn't know how much we paid for his tuition and room and board in his final year. It was about the same amount we paid for his first three years of education, so the scholarship was immaterial.

A week before graduation, I sent Brian this letter to tell him how proud I was that someone had graduated from Stanford. I had forgotten about his golf, but I felt differently about it. I did the right thing expecting a performance.

Chapter 17: 2004

Dear Brian,
June 13, 2004

Today, Brian Sinay is graduating from Stanford University. You have brought the Sinay family into this country's highest education ranks. You have single-handedly brought the Sinay family into the highest echelons of education. And it was because of your dedication to your work in school and golf. Today, I am proud of you.

Thank you for your hard work. Thank you for staying the course and working so hard for your future. Thank you for your dedication and work ethic.

This is a great accomplishment because no one in the history of the Sinay family has graduated from Stanford. You are the first. I hope you continue the tradition and get your kids there. If you marry an intelligent woman, they will have a chance to get there. They will have a chance if they get your athletic ability, too.

I hope that you will enjoy working in the world of computers. Remember that people will want to see your talent on the golf course and that it may be the ticket to your climbing up in the organization. Please remember that it is a tool that you can use to make your life better for you. Please be sure to use your golf. And, of course, I want to take you to Pebble Beach someday and play a round or two. It may be in a short time because I want to play it when my skills are still good, and I am physically healthy.

I am proud of you and wish you the best in your endeavors. Please email me about how things are going, and I will always be there for any help you need.

Love, Dad

I did not say anything about golf, and we never really talked about it again. It was done and over. There was no recovery from what had happened. Perhaps it was a perfect storm: the loss of Wally Goodwin to retirement; the inability of Brian to adjust to the methods of a new coach, essentially not something he signed up for; the lack of motivation because his goal was to get to Stanford, not perform for Stanford; the inability to handle the academics and the athletics; the unfair treatment of the coach who was not competent to be a coach for Stanford players; and his rejection as a player in his freshmen year when Wally Goodwin promised him an eleven tournament year. This was a perfect storm for the result: a suspension from the team and the elimination of his scholarship. There is never just one party at fault when something like this happens. Experiencing a bad coach at the college level has been going on since sports were invented. Sometimes these marriages just don't work out. It occurs in all sports.

On graduation day, I put this poem in a card to tell him what it meant to have a son like this and to work as hard as he did to get to Stanford and graduate. I still had this ridiculous hope that he would make some effort at his golf again. It was the hope of a father who thought his talent was wasted, but it was a talent without any desire to use it. Here is that poem.

To Brian: Graduation Day

June 20, 2000
When you were born, your eyes were wide open: I called you
  Brian.
(We were not sure of your name when you were born).
I was sleepy (it was 5 a.m.), and you were wide awake.
You were ready to take on the world; I was not as prepared as

Chapter 17: 2004

I thought I was.

When you were five, I put a little club in your hand, and you

Batted a plastic ball around the house; you also gave lots

Of hugs, played house with Jennie, and had tons of fun.

I taught you to putt at Rancho San Joaquin when you were
    six.

You also liked baseball, and you wanted to play soccer. You
    had

Fun playing and learning at school.

When you were seven, I taught you to hit a golf ball, and

You did well at it, and you wanted to do more. I kept you

Playing all the sports because you liked them all.

I never got to teach you basketball.

When you were nine, you could play golf well enough to

Enter a tournament, and you missed the cut by one stroke.

You played baseball and soccer, and you were very good at
    both.

When you were ten, you won the first of many golf.

Tournaments. You finished second in the Junior World Golf.

We went to Japan for the first of three times.

We had such fun watching you in Japan: it was super!

I never got to teach you basketball.

I taught you tennis when you were eleven, and we played
    some.

You won a ton of golf tournaments at age eleven, and we
    went to Japan

Again. You learned of a place called Stanford University
    from a

A friend and you set your sights on the goal of going there.

When you were twelve, you won the Junior World
    Championship

And we went to Japan again. It was a little redundant then.

We had fun anyway, especially with the Rosenfeld's.

When you were thirteen, you did well in your AJGA and your other

Tournaments. You met Wally Goodwin and set your sights on Stanford.

It became your goal, and you began with all A's in the seventh and eighth grades.

When you were fifteen, you entered high school an accomplished

Player. Coach Huff thought you were Mr. Cool. Well, you were

Mr. Hot, because you won the 1997 CIF High School Championship,

You joined other great first-year students named Oh, Lee, and a guy named Tiger.

When you were seventeen, you won the CIF High School Championship

Again, with a new scoring record, eclipsing the old mark of 66 set by Tiger.

It was at this time that interest in Stanford perked up. You had now won the

Championship twice; a feat few players have accomplished. You set the record

With a 65.

When you were eighteen, you tried for a third title but fell short by just

A few strokes. However, you were granted an excellent scholarship to Stanford,

And you achieved the goal you had set for yourself as a young boy. Now,

As a young man, you are on your way to a great school and future.

It was at this time that you were named again as an
   all-county player, a four
Time selection and a great accomplishment.
I never got to teach you basketball, but we did play together
   in a game!
Now, you have your future, and you can set the goals you
   want.
Your life is your life. I hope that somehow, golf will always
   be a part of your
Life, and I know that if you really put your mind to it, or
   anything else, no one has a
Chance, not even Tiger.

                Love Always,
                Dad

Despite all the heartache, I supported Brian through this challenging time. I know he did not do for me what I wanted, but it was not entirely in his control. I forgave him for that and moved on with life. Life deals us things we just never expect to happen. It is the nature of being human. Soon after his graduation, Brian got a temporary job at Google. The job quickly turned into a full-time job after about six months; now, Brian has been working for them for eighteen years. He never came home. He stayed at Stanford, bought a condo in Palo Alto with his uncle, and settled into work at Google headquarters in Mountain View, CA, just down the road. I would visit Brian at his office during the next few years. Before long, he married an Irish woman, Maeve, and had two children, James and Ruth. We never talked about Stanford golf ever again.

It was another fifteen years before Brian picked up a golf club again.

Conclusion

"A goal is not always meant to be reached; it
often serves simply as something to aim at."

Bruce Lee

Throughout the time my son and I played golf together, we
came to meet many aspiring young players who reached for
the "Golden Ring," or the chance to make it big on the PGA
Tour. We met some of the greatest players of all time in the
game of golf: Gary Players, Jack Nicklaus, and Tiger Woods,
each at the top of the ladder of golf. At the same time, my
son played with future stars on the PGA Tour like Hunter
Mahan, Aaron Baddeley, and Sergio Garcia. Like the others
in this memoir, these three looked to become the next Player,
Nicklaus, or Woods. Each of them reached for the "Golden
Ring" and a different rung of the ladder, the ladder of the best
players to play the game of golf. They all set out to become a
player on the PGA tour and flamed out at different times in
their golf careers. Some are still chasing the "Golden Ring,"
and one managed to set a record for qualifying in Q school
to play on the tour but never managed to make it successfully

enough to make a career of it. Brian was the one who had a different goal, and once that goal was reached, it was then that he became a flameout.

When each of these players reached to accomplish their goal, they ran into obstacles. In my son's case, he ran into a coaching situation different than he expected and different from what Wally Goodwin had promised. Wally had pledged to him an eleven-tournament year in his freshman year. Instead, he ran into a new coach with a new system that the coach needed to work out adequately, which resulted in a disaster. I had hoped that my son would play golf for Stanford for four years, but instead, he did not play as a team member one single time. All those fathers of the players we met during the time Brian was successful as a junior player had the hope of their sons becoming the next Jack Nicklaus or Gary Player. Each of those fathers got varying degrees of success. I wanted my son to play for Stanford and never expected him to become a PGA tour player. All I wanted was for him to play golf for Stanford.

Instead, I got heartache because he never got to play for the team at Stanford. It was my goal to see that happen. It was a difficult time in my life and a difficult time for my son. He had an obstacle that he never signed up for. It's hard to describe how challenging it is to get a young rising star to be as good as they need for competition at the highest levels. It takes devotion on the parent's side and the kid's side. Both must be committed to the goal at hand. We both were, and the goal of getting the golf scholarship was achieved. The last part of the goal was not. It is what was so difficult to accept. There was irony enough for both of us: our expectation of Brian playing eleven tournaments in his freshman year and not even playing on the team. His goal was reached, but mine was not.

Coach Mitchell was released at the end of four years, and he went back to Texas, where he came from, and coached at another college. Under Conrad Ray, Stanford's new coach, they won a couple of National Championships under his leadership and remained in the top 20 nationally ever since the removal of Coach Mitchell. Conrad Ray has been the coach since Mitchell left for eighteen years, and Stanford is a force in college golf today.

I fell off the carousel. We all have "Golden Rings" we reach for, and not all of us get what we reach for. I learned that from Bruce Lee and my son, Brian.

Acknowledgments

This book would not have happened without the help of several people. First of all, I want to thank my wife, Tina, for her loving support during the trials and tribulations of writing my first book. There is a large learning curve whenever anyone attempts to do something they have never done before and Tina's help was invaluable from giving me the alone time to do the writing, to reading and giving me feedback on the narrative, and editing my whimsical mistakes as I rushed to the end of my writing.

To my dear friends and family who took the time to read this book and offer me feedback, I am eternally grateful. Paul DiJulio, a wonderful friend, was as kind and gracious about what he discovered in the book. Sue Krenwinkle, touched by the emotion the story engendered, gave me wonderful ideas about shaping the book to an even better state. To Bill Raines, who felt mostly indifferent to the narrative, I appreciate his commentary that help shape my approach to the words I used to describe some of the dads and some of the pros in the story. Finally, my high school and Facebook friend, Catherine Clemens Sevenau, fought the same battle and gave me invaluable advice on my first publication.

To Peter Yoon and Martin Beck of the L.A. Times, whose

articles offered valuable insight into my own son's thinking, much gratitude for your excellent writing.

Finally, to my publishing team of Matt Rudnitsky at Platypus Press, who help me get the story published on Amazon, and other venues. To my copy editor, Amelia Gilliland of Vancouver, BC, Canada, for her outstanding suggestions for the editing of my work. To my Cover and Page Designer, Euan Monaghan, of The Hague, Netherlands, who formulated the design of the cover and the page layout, I am so thankful for the fantastic work.

Author Biography

Richard Sinay was a high school and college English and reading teacher for schools in Orange County, California for thirty-seven years. When he was not teaching, he was playing golf at Newport Beach Country Club and competing in club championships. He also spent time reading and writing during his career. This is his first book. He currently resides in Palm Desert, California with his wife, Tina.

Made in the USA
Monee, IL
14 January 2023

24992810R00095